SO-BDO-392

VISUAL QUICKSTART GUIDE

MACROMEDIA CONTRIBUTE 2

FOR WINDOWS AND MACINTOSH

Tom Negrino

Peachpit Press

Visual QuickStart Guide
Macromedia Contribute 2 for Windows and Macintosh
Tom Negrino

Peachpit Press
1249 Eighth Street
Berkeley, CA 94710
510/524-2178
800/283-9444
510/524-2221 (fax)

Find us on the World Wide Web at: http://www.peachpit.com/
To report errors, please send a note to errata@peachpit.com
Published by Peachpit Press, a division of Pearson Education, in association with Macromedia Press.

Copyright © 2004 by Tom Negrino

Macromedia Press Editor: Angela Kozlowski
Copyeditor: Barb Terry
Production Coordinator: Becky Winter
Compositor: Danielle Foster
Indexer: Rebecca Plunkett
Technical Review: Donald Booth
Cover Design: The Visual Group

ISBN 0-321-22849-9

9 8 7 6 5 4 3 2 1

Printed and bound in the United States of America

Dedication:

To my wife, Dori Smith, for her endless patience, her sharp technical knowledge, and her boundless support and love.

"Smart chicks are hot!"

Special Thanks to:

The folks at Peachpit

Macromedia Press/Peachpit Press acquisitions editor Wendy Sharp, who brought me in on the project and who obviously doesn't hold *Macs for Kids and Parents*, which we wrote together so long ago, against me.

My editor, Angela Kozlowski, for her keen editing.

Barb Terry, for her eagle-eyed copyediting.

Everybody else

Web designer extraordinaire Suzanne Stephens, of Stephens Design (www.stephensdesign.com), who, with design assistance from Dave Stephens, her husband and partner, created many of the Web pages used as screen-shot examples in the book. If a Web page looks good, Suzanne did it. If not, it was my fault.

The people at Macromedia: Erik Larson, senior product manager for Contribute (and technical editor for the first edition of this book); Eric Lerner, program manager; Ken Sundermeyer, Mr. Extensibility; Donald Booth (who did the technical review for this edition), Scott Unterberg; and Joann Peach.

My agent, David Rogelberg, of StudioB.

My son, Sean Smith, who put up with Cranky Dad with mostly good cheer.

Thanks to Endless River Adventures for their courtesy in allowing me to use their photos and their Web site as examples throughout this book.

The sound track for this book was graciously provided by Liz Phair, Lucy Kaplansky, Alice Peacock, Bruce Springsteen, Michelle Branch, Mary Chapin Carpenter, Warren Zevon, and, once more with feeling, the cast of Buffy the Vampire Slayer.

TABLE OF CONTENTS

TABLE OF CONTENTS

INTRODUCTION

Welcome to *Macromedia Contribute 2 for Windows and Macintosh: Visual QuickStart Guide*! Contribute 2 brings a new approach to building Web sites, promising to make life easier for both Web designers and the clients who love them.

The World Wide Web has exploded from the simple sites of its humble beginnings in the mid-1990s, when building Web pages was easy, to today's large, complex Web sites, which require skilled Web designers to create them and programmers to make the pages work together and allow visitors to interact with the site. As sites have become more complicated, they have also become more fragile; designers and programmers are reluctant to let everyday users make changes and updates to Web sites for fear that minor mistakes will cause major problems.

At the same time, the Web has become a near-ubiquitous way for companies and organizations to get their message out. The irony is that the people who most need to be able to update Web sites quickly must go through their overworked Webmasters to have changes made. In most corporations, not a day goes by when someone doesn't complain that the Web team is taking too long to add a page, change a bit of text or an image, or make other requested changes.

continues on next page

And you can't blame the Web team for serving as gatekeepers, because it's too easy for inexperienced users to mess up the links on a page and break a site.

Macromedia Contribute 2 allows designers to get back to the job of designing sites (rather than maintaining pages) and allows clients to maintain sites (rather than trying to track down the designers to make small changes). Best of all, everyone gets to do his or her job without worrying about breaking the site. With Contribute 2, anyone can safely make changes to Web sites.

The first version of Contribute ran only on Windows machines, and the biggest change for Contribute 2 is the new Mac OS X version. Along with the new Mac version comes integration with Apple's .Mac online service; you can now use Contribute 2 on the Mac to create and edit your Web pages hosted on .Mac.

What do you need?

To use Contribute, your computer needs to meet the following minimum requirements:

Windows:

- ◆ PC with a 300 MHz Intel Pentium II processor or the equivalent.

- ◆ Microsoft Windows 98 Second Edition, 2000, Me, or XP (Home or Professional).

- ◆ Microsoft Internet Explorer, version 5.0 or higher.

- ◆ At least 64 MB of RAM.

- ◆ At least 50 MB of available disk space

- ◆ A color monitor capable of 800x600-pixel resolution and able to display 256 colors.

- ◆ One of the following email clients, a requirement for the Contribute email review feature: Microsoft Outlook, Microsoft Outlook Express, Qualcomm Eudora, Netscape Communicator, or Lotus Notes.

Macintosh:

- ◆ Power Mac G3 or higher.

- ◆ Mac OS X version 10.1.5 or later

- ◆ At least 128 MB of RAM.

- ◆ At least 60 MB of available disk space

Both platforms:

- ◆ A connection to the Internet (high-speed access is strongly preferred), or access to a Web server on a local area network (LAN).

As you can see, almost any PC or Macintosh manufactured since 1998 should be able to run Contribute 2 comfortably.

What I used

The screen shots used in this book were taken on a PC running Windows XP, and a Power Mac G4 running Mac OS X 10.2.6. Screenshots from any supported version of Windows or Mac OS X should look pretty much the same as the figures in the book.

What's in the book

I've organized the different elements of building Web sites with Contribute 2 into chapters, and within each chapter are step-by-step directions that tell you exactly how to accomplish various tasks. You don't have to work through the entire book in order, but it is structured so that the more complex material builds on the easier tasks.

Throughout the book I've included many tips that will help you get things done faster, better, or both. You'll also find sidebars (with gray backgrounds) that delve deeper into subjects. Be sure to read the figure captions, too; sometimes you'll find extra nuggets of information there.

When I've listed shortcut keys, I've listed both the Windows and Macintosh equivalents, with the Mac keys in parenthesis, like so:

Ctrl-T (Cmd-T)

My assumptions about you

Writing this book, I made the assumption that you're familiar with the basics of using Windows and Mac OS X. You don't need to be a computer expert by any means, but you shouldn't be stumped by concepts like selecting text, using menus, clicking and dragging, and using files and folders.

If you're familiar with Microsoft Word and Excel, that will be helpful (especially when you get to Chapter 9, "Working with External Documents"), although it's not necessary. You should also be familiar with Web surfing and how to use a Web browser to view a Web site.

Even though you'll be using Contribute 2 to add pages and content to Web sites, you don't need to be a Web designer, Web programmer, or Web anything. Heck, you don't even have to be a good typist.

There's more help on the Web

I've prepared a companion Web site for this book, which you'll find at:

`http://www.negrino.com/contribute/`

On this site, you'll find Contribute 2 news, tips, tricks, and links to other online resources that will help you use Contribute 2 better and more productively. If I discover any mistakes in the book that somehow got through the editing process, I'll list the updates on the site, too.

Let's get started

Macromedia Contribute 2 is a new kind of software, one that allows people who don't want to have to deal with HTML, JavaScript, CSS, or any other Web technology to put their Web sites back into their own hands and get their thoughts and work onto the Web. It does this not by bypassing Web professionals but by forging partnerships with them. Contribute 2 offers exciting possibilities for everyone who wants to express themselves on the Web.

So now, on with the book!

Tom Negrino

July 2003

INTRODUCTION

GETTING STARTED

Welcome to Macromedia Contribute 2! With Contribute, you'll be able to easily add content to Web sites, with a minimum of hassle and complexity. You'll still need to know a little bit about how the Web works, but for the most part, as long as you can use a word processor (such as Microsoft Word), you'll be able to build Web pages with Contribute.

Contribute allows you to add new pages, text, images, Macromedia Flash animations, and more to your Web sites. With Contribute's built-in Web browser, you can view pages on your sites (or anywhere on the Web). On Web sites you are allowed to change, you can edit individual pages and then send the draft copies of those pages to your coworkers by email for approval, or you can publish your changes directly to the Web site.

continues on next page

Contribute works hand-in-hand with Dreamweaver MX, Macromedia's powerful Web design program. Designers can create page templates in Dreamweaver, and those templates can then be used by Contribute. But Contribute isn't just friendly with Dreamweaver and other Macromedia products; it plays well with others, too. You can drag Microsoft Word or Excel documents into Contribute, and publish them easily and immediately on the Web. In fact, Contribute can work with documents from almost any other program.

In this chapter you'll learn how to install and run Contribute for both Windows and Macintosh, and you'll get a look at Contribute's work space and user interface. Most important, I'll introduce you to Contribute's *workflow*, the sequence of events that let you create and edit Web pages.

Installing and Running Contribute

Like most programs, Contribute provides step-by-step instructions for installation as soon as you insert the CD-ROM into your computer. Here's a bit of guidance to help you get the application up and running.

About Product Activation

New to Contribute 2 is *product activation*, which is a one-time process that authenticates licensed users during the installation process (on Macintosh, activation occurs the first time you run the program). The process verifies that the serial number is legitimate, and has not been activated on more systems than allowed by the Macromedia End User License Agreement (EULA). For more information about the Contribute license terms, see the "New Licensing" sidebar.

During product activation, the Contribute 2 installer creates two unique codes, one based on some of the information about your computer's hardware, and the other based on a large random number. This information, along with your Contribute serial number, is combined, encrypted, and then sent to Macromedia for verification via the Internet (or you can use a toll-free telephone number). Macromedia says that they are sensitive to privacy concerns, and promises that none of the collected information can be used to identify you or your individual hardware components in any way. You can transfer your activation from one computer to another, so if you upgrade your machine, you can easily deactivate the software on your old computer, then reactivate it on your new computer. If you need more information about product activation, see http://www.macromedia.com/go/activation/.

continues on next page

- If your company or organization has purchased a site license for Contribute 2, you will not have to go through product activation. If you choose not to activate your copy of Contribute (because, say, you've downloaded Contribute 2 from the Macromedia Web site to check it out and you don't have a serial number yet), the Contribute installer will install the program in a fully-functional trial mode, which expires after 30 days and stops working. You can purchase and enter a serial number and activate the product at any time during the trial period.

Right after activation, you'll have the opportunity to also register the product with Macromedia online. This allows the company to (if you agree) contact you about updates to Contribute and their other products. Macromedia says that there's no connection between product activation and product registration.

There is an optional installation with Contribute 2: the Paypal Ecommerce Toolkit. This gives you tools that allow you to create buttons on your Web pages that work with the PayPal online payment service. You can use these buttons to let visitors to your site purchase products or subscriptions, or give your site a shopping cart. If you are interested in this capability, I suggest that you install the toolkit now. You can install it later, but you will have to reinstall Contribute as well; easier to do it all now.

New Licensing

With the previous version of Contribute, the user license allowed you to use Contribute on only one computer. However, there was nothing to prevent you from installing the program on both your desktop machine and your laptop (although if they were on the same network and you attempted to run Contribute simultaneously on both machines, the second copy would detect the first copy and refuse to launch). With the advent of product activation in Contribute 2, the copy of Contribute is associated with the particular computer it is installed on, and if you try to run Contribute on more machines than you are licensed for, the program will refuse to run.

This posed obvious problems for people who do their work on both a desktop and laptop computer, and rather than attempting to force you to purchase a second copy of Contribute, Macromedia has changed the Contribute license terms so that you can install the program on a second machine, such as a laptop or a home machine. The restriction is that both copies of Contribute can't be running at the same time. This license flexibility should allow most people to use Contribute at work, and also at home or on the road, without violating the user license, and without the legal requirement to purchase more copies of Contribute than they really need.

Figure 1.1 Double-click the Macromedia Contribute shortcut icon on your desktop to get started with the program.

To install Macromedia Contribute on Windows:

1. Insert the Contribute CD-ROM in your CD drive.

   The Contribute Installer automatically launches.

2. Follow the onscreen instructions to install and activate the program.

   During the installation, you'll need to enter your serial number, which you'll find in the box; you can also get it from your site administrator if your company has licensed multiple copies of Contribute.

3. When the installation is complete, eject the Contribute CD-ROM.

   If you selected the options during installation, the Installer leaves behind a shortcut icon on your desktop (**Figure 1.1**), and there may also be a Contribute icon in the Quick Launch section of the Taskbar.

To install Macromedia Contribute on Macintosh:

1. Insert the Contribute CD-ROM in your CD drive.

   The Contribute CD appears on your desktop.

2. Double-click the CD to open it, then double-click to start the Contribute 2 Installer application.

3. Follow the onscreen instructions to install and activate the program.

   The program will by default be installed into your Applications folder.

4. When the installation is complete, quit the Installer, then eject the Contribute CD-ROM by dragging it to the Trash.

INSTALLING AND RUNNING CONTRIBUTE

To run Contribute for the first time:

If you are connected to the Internet, the first time you run Contribute, the program will prompt you to register with Macromedia. Since Contribute has a built-in Web browser, this is an easy process. After you finish registering, Contribute will display its Welcome screen (**Figure 1.2**).

The Welcome screen helps you learn about Contribute, and offers you a link to create a site connection. You'll learn more about creating site connections in Chapter 2, "Making a Site Connection."

◆ Double-click the Contribute 2 icon on your desktop.

   or

   Choose Start > Programs > Macromedia > Macromedia Contribute 2.

◆ On Macintosh, double-click the Contribute icon in the `Applications/ Macromedia Contribute 2` folder.

● The first time the program runs, you'll need to enter your serial number, which you'll find in the box; you can also get it from your site administrator if your company has licensed multiple copies of Contribute. After entering the serial number, Contribute performs the product activation process, and then offers you the opportunity to register over the Internet.

Figure 1.2 Contribute's Welcome screen lets you learn more about the program, or lets you create a connection to your Web site.

Exploring the Contribute Work Space

In Contribute everything happens in one window; unlike other Web tools such as Dreamweaver, Contribute has no separate tool palettes, property inspectors, or other windows you need to manage. Instead, you get an uncluttered, clean interface (**Figure 1.3**).

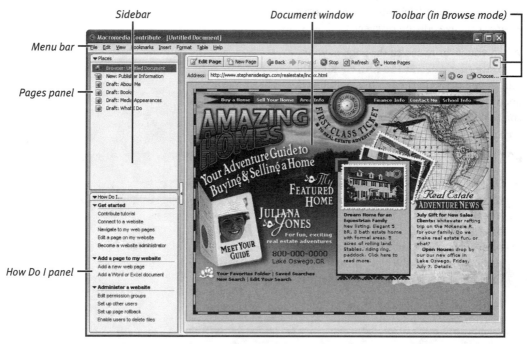

Figure 1.3 The Macromedia Contribute environment: The document window is in Browse mode, and the Browser toolbar is displayed.

The document window

Most of your work is done in Contribute's document window. You use the document window to browse to pages you want to edit. The document window works like any other Web browser; in fact, it is actually an embedded version of Microsoft Internet Explorer (on Windows) or Opera 6 (on Macintosh). You can use Contribute's built-in browser to view any Web page, but you can only edit pages in your own Web sites—that is, sites where you have editing privileges.

When you've browsed to the page in your Web site that you want to edit, clicking the Edit Page button in the toolbar switches the document window into Edit mode, allowing you to add or change text or graphic elements on the page.

✔ Tip

■ On Windows, the Contribute Web browser gets its preferences from your system's Internet Explorer browser. To change settings such as fonts or to enable plug-ins such as Flash or QuickTime, change the settings or install the plug-ins in Internet Explorer, then relaunch Contribute.

The toolbars

Contribute has two toolbars, the Browser toolbar and the Editing toolbar.

When you're in Browse mode, Contribute displays the Browser toolbar, which contains an abbreviated set of the familiar Web-browser controls, such as Back, Forward, Stop, and Refresh buttons, and an Address field, where you can type the URL of a page you want to browse (**Figure 1.4**). When you're browsing sites where you have editing privileges, the Browser toolbar also contains Edit Page and New Page buttons. When you're browsing sites where you don't yet have editing privileges, these two buttons are replaced by a single Create Connection button. Clicking this button starts up the process of making a site connection, which is required before you can edit the site. See Chapter 2, "Making a Site Connection," for more information. In some situations, the Browser toolbar may also show the *info bar*, which gives you more information about the page you're browsing.

Figure 1.4 The Browser toolbar works just like Internet Explorer's, with the addition of the Edit Page and New Page buttons, and sometimes the info bar, as shown.

✔ Tip

- Blue text in the info bar is a hyperlink; you can click it to go to the page that the info bar is telling you about.

When editing a page, you'll see the Editing toolbar, which contains buttons and pop-up menus for common editing operations (**Figure 1.5**). Many of these controls replicate choices from the Insert, Format, and Table menus. You'll also see the Publish, Save for Later, and Cancel buttons, which allow you to publish the draft page you're working on to your Web site, save the draft for additional editing later, or cancel editing altogether.

The Browser and Editing toolbars look virtually identical on the Windows and Mac versions of Contribute.

PayPal ecommerce extension (optional)

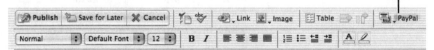

Figure 1.5 The Editing toolbar contains tools to add and edit Web page elements.

Figure 1.6 The sidebar's Pages panel allows you to switch between Browse and Edit modes, and lists new or draft pages.

Figure 1.7 The How Do I panel shows common tasks, for which it has step-by-step instructions.

Figure 1.8 An example of Contribute's step-by-step instructions.

The sidebar

Contribute's main navigation tool is the *sidebar*. The sidebar also gives you quick access to brief tutorials on how to accomplish specific tasks. It has two panes:

◆ The Pages panel allows you to switch between the built-in browser and any new or draft pages you have open (**Figure 1.6**). When you click Browser in the Pages panel, you can browse to any page on the Internet, and that page is displayed in the document window. You can click any draft or new page listed in the Pages panel, and the document window switches to Edit mode and allows you to edit the page. Because all your editing operations in Contribute occur in the document window, the Pages panel takes the place of the Window menu found in many other Windows applications.

◆ The How Do I panel provides quick instructions to help you complete common tasks (**Figure 1.7**). The list of tasks changes, depending on whether you're browsing or editing. In either case, clicking a task displays more information on how to accomplish it (**Figure 1.8**). Some How Do I topics provide several layers of instructions; keep selecting until you get to the instructions you need.

✔ Tip

■ The Pages and How Do I panels are resizable. You can double-click the heading of either panel to collapse it, or you can drag the header of the How Do I panel up or down to adjust the size of either panel in the sidebar. Once you get used to using Contribute, you might want to collapse the How Do I panel altogether, especially to make room for new or draft pages in the Pages panel. You can also drag the border between the sidebar and the document to change their width.

EXPLORING THE CONTRIBUTE WORK SPACE

Getting Onscreen Help

Contribute's onscreen help is based on the standard help systems for Windows and Mac OS X. Not surprisingly, you access the help files via the program's Help menu (**Figure 1.9**).

To get onscreen help (Windows):

1. Choose Help > Macromedia Contribute Help, or press F1.

   The Contribute Help window opens (**Figure 1.10**).

2. On the Contents tab, click the book icons to browse to the Help topic you want. The detailed documentation appears on the right side of the window.

   or

   Select the Search tab, type a search keyword, and click the List Topics button. The list of found topics appears in the "Select Topic to display" box. Click the topic you want, then click Display. The documentation appears on the right side of the window.

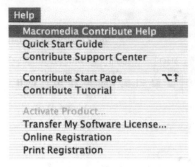

Figure 1.9 The Help menu gives you access to a variety of help and support resources.

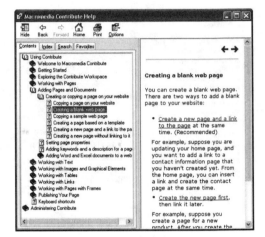

Figure 1.10 To use Contribute's online help on Windows, you can either browse or search by keyword.

GETTING ONSCREEN HELP

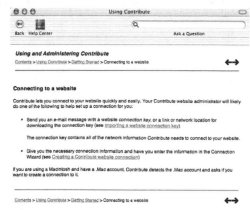

Figure 1.11 Contribute offers help using the standard Help Viewer on Mac OS X.

To get onscreen help (Mac):

1. Choose Help > Macromedia Contribute Help, or press the Help key.

The Help Viewer application launches, and the Contribute Help window opens.

2. Click the help topics to browse to the Help topic you want. The detailed documentation appears on the right side of the window (**Figure 1.11**).

or

Click in the Ask a Question field, type a search keyword, and press Return. The list of found topics appears in the window. Click the topic you want. The documentation appears in the window.

Understanding Contribute's Workflow

In order to get the most out of using Macromedia Contribute, you need to understand how Contribute approaches the task of creating and editing Web pages. Other Web site tools, even Macromedia's own Dreamweaver, are largely built around the concept that one person, or perhaps a team of people, has full access to a Web site, with the unfettered ability to make changes throughout the site. In contrast, Contribute presumes that one or more *site administrators* are responsible for managing a Web site, and one or more groups of users are able to add content to the site but have little or no need to deal with the site's design or its HTML or other code. For these content contributors, Contribute makes adding information to a Web site as easy as using a word processor such as Microsoft Word, but in part accomplishes this ease of use by limiting the ability of contributors to make design changes to the site.

The administrator's workflow

The Contribute administrator is responsible for setting up the connections to Web sites and defining what changes a user or group of users are allowed to make to the site. These *permissions* might, for example, allow a group called "Reporters" to create and edit pages, but not delete pages, a privilege reserved for the "Editors" group. Similarly, the "Copy-editors" group could be restricted to only editing text and changing its formatting.

Permission groups are created by the site administrator and distributed to the different user groups, via email or over a network, as part of a file called a *connection key*. The connection key, which is encrypted and protected by a password, contains the information the user needs to connect to the Web site over the local network or the Internet, and also contains that user's site permissions. To add the new site connection to his or her copy of Contribute, the user simply double-clicks a connection key file. For more information on creating connection files, see Chapter 2. See Chapter 10, "Site Administration," for more information on setting up permission groups.

✔ Tips

■ There can be more than one site administrator, and a group can share the administrative duties.

■ The site administrator can create a permission group that restricts editing to only specific folders. This is an especially useful capability because, for example, the administrator can keep the Marketing department out of Human Resources' Web pages, and vice versa.

■ Administrators, by definition, have complete control over the Web site. The site administrator could also be one of the users, or perhaps the only user.

■ A site administrator can use Contribute or Macromedia Dreamweaver MX, which includes the same administration tools found in Contribute.

UNDERSTANDING CONTRIBUTE'S WORKFLOW

The contributor's workflow

As a contributor to a Web site, before you can begin editing pages, you must import or create a connection to the Web server. Most of the time, your Web-site administrator creates a connection key for you. To learn more about importing site connections, see Chapter 2. Once you've set up the site connection, there are three steps to editing any existing Web page in Contribute:

◆ First you **browse** to the page you want to edit using Contribute's built-in Web browser.

◆ You then **edit** the page using Contribute's editing tools. If you are editing an existing page, Contribute makes a draft copy of the page for you to work on. Contribute also locks the page so that no one can modify this page at the same time you're working on it.

◆ Finally, you **publish** the draft page to your Web site.

Understanding this **browse-edit-publish** workflow is the key to working with Web pages in Contribute.

Building new pages

Of course, you can also create new pages with Contribute, either from a new blank page, new pages based on *Dreamweaver templates*, or pages based on *non-Dreamweaver templates*.

Dreamweaver templates allow the page designer to create the page and designate portions of it as editable. The rest of the page is locked to the Contribute user. This ability to lock portions of a page is a great solution to the problem of users' inadvertently messing up page designs. The site administrator can specify which user groups have access to specific templates. When you create a new page from a Dreamweaver template, Contribute makes a copy of the template page and allows you to work only within the editable regions.

Non-Dreamweaver templates are pages that are completely editable and can be used as models for new pages. When you create a new page from one of these templates, Contribute makes a copy of the page, and you make your changes to the copy. As with Dreamweaver templates, the site administrator can specify user access. Contribute's Sample Pages are non-Dreamweaver templates. See Chapter 3 for more about Sample Pages.

UNDERSTANDING CONTRIBUTE'S WORKFLOW

Setting a Startup Password

One of the new features in Contribute 2 is the ability to set a password that you must enter when you start up the program. This helps prevent changes to your Web sites by anyone that sits down at your computer. If you enable a startup password, the connection information on your machine will also be encrypted to provide extra security.

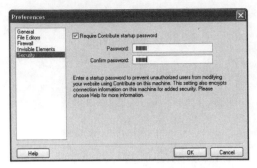

Figure 1.12 Type a password to make Contribute secure from mischief-makers.

To set a startup password:

1. Choose Edit > Preferences (Contribute > Preferences).

   The Preferences dialog appears.

2. Click the Security category.

   The Security panel appears (**Figure 1.12**)

3. Select "Require Contribute startup password."

4. Type a password in the "Password" field, then type it again in the "Confirm password" field.

5. Click OK.

SETTING A STARTUP PASSWORD

Making a
Site Connection

Although it is possible to edit pages with Macromedia Contribute 2 that are not on a Web server (this is called *offline editing*), chances are you will be using Contribute to create and edit pages over an Internet or local area network (LAN) connection to a Web server. The server could be the machine running your live Web site, sometimes called the *production server*, or it could be a test server, also known as a *staging server*. A staging server is usually used for editing and review of a site's pages where several people must approve the design and content before the site or page goes live on the Internet.

Regardless of whether you use a production or a staging server, you need to tell Contribute how to connect to the server before you can start working on pages. Contribute's Connection Wizard (on Macintosh, the Connection Assistant) walks you through the connection process. Once you have connected to your Web site, you can use Contribute to edit files, make new files, and if you are an administrator, create files called *connection keys*, which contain all the information needed to make a server connection with Contribute. You can share your connection keys with other people. All they have to do is import the connection key you send them, and they can connect to your site and start editing pages without needing to fiddle with connection settings themselves.

Preparing to Connect

Contribute can connect to your Web server in three ways. The more common connection, called *FTP* (see the sidebar "What's FTP?"), is used when your server resides on the Internet or on your company's intranet. The other way to connect is over your company's *local area network* (LAN). The third way is new to Contribute 2, and is called *SFTP*, for Secure FTP.

Before you begin creating an FTP or SFTP connection, you need to ask your network administrator for some information about the Web server you're using. You will need:

◆ Your name and email address

◆ The Web site address, which is usually in the form http://www.mysite.com

◆ The connection type, which will be either FTP, SFTP, or Local/Network

◆ The FTP or SFTP address for your server

◆ The log-in name for the FTP or SFTP server

◆ The password associated with the log-in name

◆ The folder's path on the FTP or SFTP server that contains your Web site

Once you have all this information in hand, you're ready to use Contribute's Connection Wizard (or on Macintosh, the Connection Assistant) to set up your FTP or SFTP connection with the Web site you'll be working on.

When connecting to a Web site using a Local/Network connection, you only need to know the location, or *network path*, of the folder that holds your Web site. You can locate the folder on your network using the Choose button in the Connection Wizard as described later in this chapter.

What's FTP and SFTP?

If you've never done any Web site maintenance before, you might be baffled by the term *FTP*. It stands for "File Transfer Protocol," and is a common method for transferring files (such as Web pages and images) between two computers connected to the Internet. Web servers often use FTP to send files between the server and the computer of whomever is maintaining the Web site. In order to do this, the server machine runs an *FTP server* program in addition to the Web server software. Normally you need a program called an *FTP client* on your computer in order to transfer files to and from an FTP server. Web page creation programs such as Contribute and Macromedia Dreamweaver have the FTP client functions built in.

One of the drawbacks to FTP is that it is a protocol with no built-in security; all information is sent "in the clear," including your username, password, and the files themselves. The Secure FTP (SFTP) protocol solves this problem by encrypting all information sent between the SFTP client (in this case, Contribute 2) and the SFTP server.

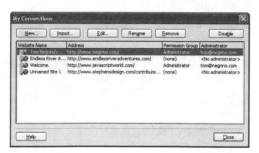

Figure 2.1 The My Connections window is where you manage all of your connection information.

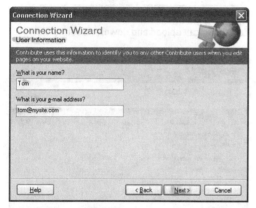

Figure 2.2 In the User Information screen, you enter the name and email address for the connection.

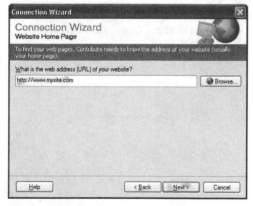

Figure 2.3 Entering the URL of your Web site in the Website Home Page screen allows Contribute to find your site for editing.

Using the Connection Wizard (Windows)

Connecting to a Web site can be a little intimidating, so Contribute for Windows provides an easy-to-use Connection Wizard, which walks you through the process. You can start the Connection Wizard by clicking the "Create a connection" link in Contribute's Welcome screen, which appears after you first install the program.

To make a site connection

1. Choose Edit > My Connections.

   The My Connections window appears (**Figure 2.1**).

2. Click the New button.

   The Connection Wizard starts up and displays a welcome screen.

3. Click Next. The User Information screen appears.

4. Type your name, press Tab, then type your email address (**Figure 2.2**). Click Next.

   The Website Home Page screen appears (**Figure 2.3**).

continues on next page

USING THE CONNECTION WIZARD (WINDOWS)

5. Enter the address of your Web site. It's important to provide the entire Web address, so be sure to include the `http://` portion of the address. Click Next.

6. You'll perform several steps on the Connection Information screen (**Figure 2.4**).

   If you use FTP as your connection method, choose FTP from the pop-up menu and skip to step 9.

   or

   If you use SFTP as your connection method, choose Secure FTP (SFTP) from the pop-up menu and skip to step 9.

   or

   Choose Local/Network from the pop-up menu. The Connection Information screen changes to reflect your choice (**Figure 2.5**).

7. Click the Choose button next to "What is the network path to your website?"

   In the resulting "Select Website Path" dialog, navigate to the location of your Web site in the usual Windows fashion. This network path must lead to the web server. Check with your site administrator for the exact path if you are unsure.

8. Click the Next button, and skip to step 13.

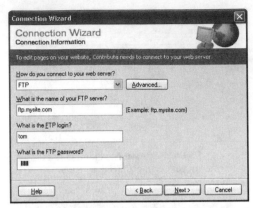

Figure 2.4 Enter your FTP server information so that Contribute can upload and download edited files.

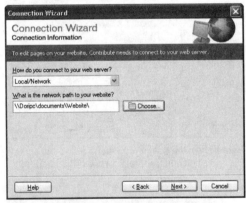

Figure 2.5 If you are editing pages on your local network, you must give Contribute the network path to the Web site.

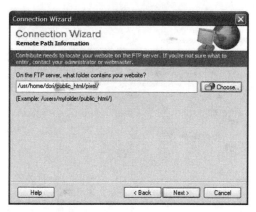

Figure 2.6 In the Remote Path Information screen you specify the folder on your Web server where your Web site resides.

9. Enter the FTP or SFTP address for your server, then press Tab.

10. Enter your FTP or SFTP log-in name, then press Tab.

11. Enter your FTP or SFTP password, then click Next.

    The Remote Path Information screen appears. There will be a delay before this screen appears, while a Testing Connection progress dialog displays. This is normal; Contribute is verifying that the FTP or SFTP information is valid. If there's a problem, an alert dialog will appear.

12. Enter the path to the folder on the FTP or SFTP server that contains your Web site (**Figure 2.6**). Click Next.

    This is where you are most likely to have problems, because the path that appears in a Web browser's Address line for a site is often not the actual path used by the Web server, which is what you need. Contribute will attempt to determine the right path to your site, but in some cases, you will have to enter it yourself. You'll need to get the actual path from your Webmaster or network administrator, or use the Choose button to browse to the correct folder.

    continues on next page

USING THE CONNECTION WIZARD (WINDOWS)

13. The Administrator Information screen asks if you want to become the administrator for this site (**Figure 2.7**). Select the Yes button, enter the administrator password for the site, and enter it again to confirm. This screen will only be displayed if no one has already set up Contribute administration for your site. Then click Next. If a Contribute site administrator has previously been established, you will be prompted to choose a User Group.

or

Click the No button, then click Next.

14. The Summary screen confirms that you have successfully made the connection, and summarizes all the information you entered (**Figure 2.8**). Click Done.

✔ Tip

■ You can set yourself up as the site administrator without an administrator password. Just don't enter anything in the password fields in step 13. A dialog opens, confirming that you really don't want an administrator password. The drawback to not having an administrator password is that any Contribute user of the site will be able to change the permissions for the site. See Chapter 10, "Site Administration," for more information on working with permissions and administering Contribute sites.

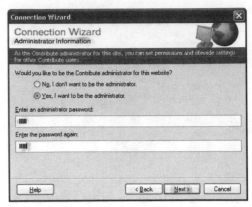

Figure 2.7 In the Administrator Information screen you can designate yourself as the site's administrator.

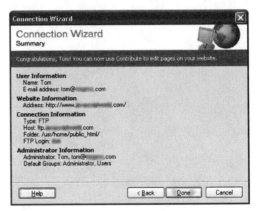

Figure 2.8 The Summary screen allows you to review the information you entered. I've blurred some sensitive information in this screenshot.

Figure 2.9 The Mac's My Connection dialog is where you begin creating a new connection.

Figure 2.10 Type your name and email address in the User Info screen of the Connection Assistant.

Figure 2.11 Tell Contribute the location of your Web site by entering the URL of your site in the Website Home Page screen.

Using the Connection Assistant (Macintosh)

The equivalent of the Contribute Connection Wizard on Windows is the Connection Assistant on Macintosh. It steps you through the process of creating connection keys for your Web sites.

To make a site connection

1. Choose Contribute > My Connections.

   The My Connections window appears (**Figure 2.9**).

2. Click the New button.

   The Connection Wizard starts up and displays an Introduction screen.

3. Click Continue. The User Info screen appears.

4. Type your name, press Tab, then type your email address (**Figure 2.10**). Click Continue.

   The Web site Home Page screen appears (**Figure 2.11**).

continues on next page

USING THE CONNECTION ASSISTANT (MACINTOSH)

5. Enter the address of your Web site. It's important to provide the entire Web address, so be sure to include the `http://` portion of the address.

or

You can browse to your Web site by clicking the Browse button in the Web site Home Page screen, which brings up a browser dialog (**Figure 2.12**). Browse to the page that you want, then click OK to return to the Web site Home Page screen. Click Continue.

6. You'll perform several steps on the Connection Info screen (**Figure 2.13**).

If you use FTP as your connection method, choose FTP from the pop-up menu and skip to step 14.

or

If you use SFTP as your connection method, choose Secure FTP (SFTP) from the pop-up menu and skip to step 14.

or

Choose Local/Network from the pop-up menu. The Connection Info screen changes to reflect your choice (**Figure 2.14**).

7. For Local/Network connections, the disk which contains the Web server must be mounted on your desktop. Switch to the Finder by clicking on your desktop.

Figure 2.12 You can browse to the page you want for the Connection Assistant with the built-in browser dialog.

Figure 2.13 Enter your FTP server information.

Figure 2.14 If you are editing pages on your local network, enter the network path to the Web site.

Figure 2.15 Select the disk containing the local Web site.

Figure 2.16 The icon of the network disk appears on your desktop.

8. In the Finder, choose Go > Connect to Server, or press Cmd-K.

The Connect to Server dialog appears (**Figure 2.15**).

9. Click to select a network in the left column, then click to select a server name in the next column to the right.

10. Click Connect.

The icon of the server appears on your desktop (**Figure 2.16**).

11. Switch back to Contribute.

The Connection Info screen reappears.

12. Click the Browse button next to "What is the network path to your website?"

In the resulting "Select Website Path" dialog, navigate to the location of your Web site, then click Choose. The Connection Info screen reappears. You can navigate to the site location by dragging the icon of the mounted server to the path field.

13. Click the Continue button, and skip to step 18.

14. Enter the FTP or SFTP address for your server, then press Tab.

15. Enter your FTP or SFTP log-in name, then press Tab.

16. Enter your FTP or SFTP password, then click Continue.

The Remote Path Info screen appears. There will be a delay before this screen appears, while a Testing Connection progress dialog displays. This is normal; Contribute is verifying that the FTP or SFTP information is valid. If there's a problem, an alert dialog will appear.

continues on next page

Missing Connections

You might have noticed that Contribute isn't as flexible as Dreamweaver at providing ways to connect to Web sites. Of Dreamweaver's six connection choices, Contribute does not offer four: None (Contribute requires that you edit pages on a server); RDS (Contribute can only edit pages residing on a ColdFusion server using FTP or Local/Network connections); SourceSafe Database (Contribute doesn't connect to databases); and WebDAV (Contribute only supports this protocol with .Mac accounts on the Mac).

USING THE CONNECTION ASSISTANT (MACINTOSH)

17. Enter the path to the folder on the FTP or SFTP server that contains your Web site (**Figure 2.17**). Click Next.

This is where you are most likely to have problems, because the path that appears in a Web browser's Address line for a site is often not the actual path used by the Web server, which is what you need. Contribute will attempt to determine the right path to your site, but in some cases, you will have to enter it yourself. You'll need to get the actual path from your Webmaster or network administrator, or use the Choose button to browse to the correct folder.

18. The Administrator Information screen asks if you want to become the administrator for this site. Select the Yes button, enter the administrator password for the site, and enter it again to confirm. This screen will only be displayed if no one has already set up Contribute administration for your site. Then click Next.

or

Click the No button, then click Next.

19. The Summary screen confirms that you have successfully made the connection, and summarizes all the information you entered (**Figure 2.18**). Click Done.

✔ Tips

■ You can start the Connection Assistant by clicking the "Create a connection" link in Contribute's Welcome screen, which appears after you first install the program.

Figure 2.17 Specify the folder on your Web server where your Web site resides.

Figure 2.18 The Summary screen allows you to review the information you entered, and you can go back and fix mistakes. I've blurred some sensitive information in this screenshot.

➕ ■ Connection keys for Local/Network connections will not work across platforms, because Macs and Windows use different ways to specify network paths. You should recreate such connections on each platform. A Macintosh must create a connection key for Local/Network connections that will be used by other Mac users. Windows users will have to receive a connection key created on Windows.

USING THE CONNECTION ASSISTANT (MACINTOSH)

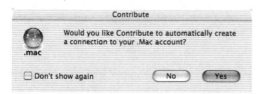

Figure 2.19 The first time you launch Contribute, it will ask if you want to set up a connection to your .Mac account.

Figure 2.20 Access the .Mac connection from the Home Pages pop-up menu.

Connecting to a .Mac Account (Mac-only)

If you have a .Mac account, you probably already know that one of the features of that account is Home Page, a Web server that can contain one or more Web sites that you create. Contribute 2 can create a connection key to your .Mac account, and best of all, Contribute does the job automatically. When you first launch Contribute 2 for Mac OS X, the program detects your .Mac account information from the Internet panel of System Preferences, and creates a connection key.

To connect to a .Mac account:

1. Launch Contribute 2 for Mac OS X.

2. If you have a .Mac account, Contribute asks if you want to create a connection to that account (**Figure 2.19**).

3. Click Yes.

   Contribute makes the connection key.

To edit .Mac pages:

1. From the Browser toolbar, choose .Mac Connection from the Home Pages pop-up menu (**Figure 2.20**).

   or

   Choose View > Home Pages > .Mac Connection.

   or

   Choose Help > Contribute Start page, then click .Mac Connection under "Begin editing my websites."

2. Edit your pages (or create new pages) in the usual fashion. See Chapter 3, "Building Web Pages," for more information.

✔ Tips

- Mac OS X uses the WebDAV protocol to mount your iDisk on the Finder's desktop. When you make a connection key to your .Mac account, Contribute calls on the OS X Finder to mount the iDisk.

- There are several quirks about editing pages on the .Mac servers that you should be aware of. For example, pages that you edit using the .Mac tools (such as Home Page or iPhoto slide shows) are generated by the .Mac server software, and so aren't good candidates for changing with Contribute. But there's no problem in creating other pages with Contribute. Before you do a lot of work with Contribute and your .Mac account, be sure to read the "Using Contribute with a .Mac account" Tech Note on Macromedia's support site. You can find that Tech Note at <http://www.macromedia.com/support/contribute/ts/documents/dot_mac.htm >.

- Contribute for Mac OS X needs to have Local/Network disks mounted on the desktop. Contribute also verifies every active connection when it launches. So if you have a .Mac connection defined in Contribute, every time that you start the program, your iDisk will mount on the desktop. If you want to avoid this, you can temporarily disable the .Mac connection (see the "Disabling Site Connections" sidebar later in this chapter).

Figure 2.21 You'll need to enter the site administrator password to begin the sharing process.

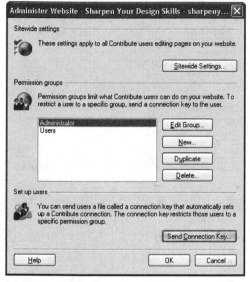

Figure 2.22 Click the Send Connection Key button to start the Export Wizard.

Sharing Site Connections

After you have created a site connection, you can save it as a file to your hard drive or email it to coworkers. Recipients of this *connection key* can import it into their copy of Contribute and immediately use it to make a connection and start editing pages without having to go through the connection setup process themselves.

Through Contribute's Permission Groups feature, you, as the site administrator, can limit the editing abilities of the recipients of your connection keys. Why might this be a good idea? Consider a situation in which you have a team (even a small team) working on a particular Web site, say a site for a community organization. You might want people assigned to update the News section of your site to be able to access pages only in the news folder, or you might want them to be able to modify existing pages but not create new pages. The Contribute site administrator can prepare and distribute different connection keys that specify the level of access allowed by team members. See Chapter 10, "Site Administration" for more information about permissions.

The Windows version of Contribute uses an Export Wizard to step you through the process of sending the connection key; the Mac equivalent is called the Export Assistant. They work virtually identically; I've called out the few differences in the following steps.

To share a connection key via email:

1. Choose Edit > Administer Websites (Contribute > Administer Websites), then choose the Web site you want from the hierarchical menu. Contribute asks you to enter the site administrator's password (**Figure 2.21**).

2. Enter the password and click OK. The Administer Website window opens (**Figure 2.22**).

continues on next page

3. Click the Send Connection Key button. The first screen of the Export Wizard (Export Assistant) appears (**Figure 2.23**).

4. Make sure the Yes button is selected, then click Next.

(Optional) Click the "Include my FTP login and password" checkbox.

If you want to include your log-in information in the key, check this; if the person you're sending the key to has his or her own FTP log-in, leave this option unchecked.

Note that if you choose No, Contribute will allow you to customize the connection settings before you create the export file. See Chapter 10 for more information about customizing connection settings.

5. The Group Information screen appears (**Figure 2.24**). Select the permission group you want for the connection file you're creating, then click Next.

6. The Connection Key Information screen opens (**Figure 2.25**). Choose whether to send the connection file in an email or save it to disk. Then enter the password or pass phrase for the connection file, repeat the password or pass phrase for verification, and click Next.

Contribute encrypts the connection key with the password or pass phrase so that it can't be opened except by the intended recipient.

7. The Summary screen of the Export Wizard appears, allowing you to review the information. If you need to make changes, click Back. Otherwise, click Done.

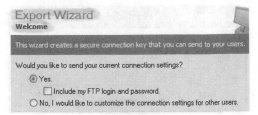

Figure 2.23 You can either send the connection file as is, or edit it before sending.

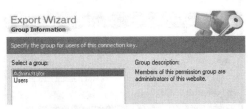

Figure 2.24 If you have specified permission groups, you can assign a group to the exported connection key.

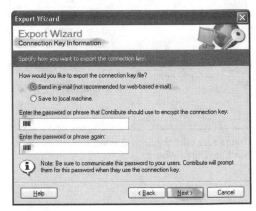

Figure 2.25 You can send a connection key file by email or save it to your hard drive, but either way, you must assign it a password.

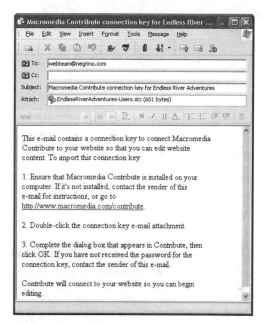

Figure 2.26 Contribute automatically creates an outgoing message in your email program (in this case, it's Microsoft Outlook Express for Windows), with the connection key file as an attachment.

Figure 2.27 Use the Export Connection Key dialog to save the file to your hard drive.

8. If you chose to send the connection key by email, Contribute launches your email program and create a new message with the connection key as an attachment, with the subject already filled in, and with instructions in the body of the message (**Figure 2.26**). Address the message, make any other changes you want, and send the mail on its way.

or

If you chose to save the connection key to disk, the Export Connection Key dialog appears (**Figure 2.27**). Choose the location on your hard drive or local network for the connection key, and click Save.

✔ Tips

- You must enter a password or pass phrase to protect exported connection keys. Contribute won't allow you to create unprotected files.

- If you email a connection key to a co-worker, you must make sure that he or she also receives the password or pass phrase for the file. But it will defeat the purpose of the protection if you include the password in the body of the email. Always communicate the password to the recipient in a separate communication, for example via fax, in a different email, or even by telephone. Shouting the password over cubicle walls is not considered to be a high-security solution!

- Contribute uses your default email program, as set on the Programs tab of the Internet Properties control panel (Windows) or the Email tab of the internet panel of System Preferences (Mac), to send email. It is not recommended that a Web-based email client, such as Hotmail, be used, as it may corrupt the key.

Importing Site Connection Keys

When you receive a connection key, you need to import it into Contribute in order to use the file and make the connection.

To import a connection key:

1. Choose Edit > My Connections (Contribute > My Connections). The My Connections dialog appears.

2. Click the Import button. The Select Connection Key dialog appears (**Figure 2.28**).

3. Navigate to the connection key on your hard drive, select the key file, and click Open or press Enter (Return).

4. The Import Connection Key dialog appears (**Figure 2.29**). If necessary, enter your name and email address, then enter the password or pass phrase for the connection key. Click OK.

✔ Tips

- There's a faster way to import connection keys. Simply double-click on the connection key file which brings up the Import Connection Key dialog.

- If you attempt to import a connection key and you already have a connection for that site listed in your My Connections dialog, Contribute asks if you want to replace the old settings file with the site settings you're importing. Contribute only allows one connection per site per user.

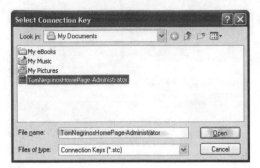

Figure 2.28 Use the Select Connection Key dialog to import connection keys to your hard drive and to open them.

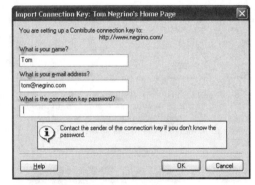

Figure 2.29 To import a connection key, enter your name, email address, and password in the Import Connection Key dialog.

Editing Site Connections

On occasion, you'll need to edit a site connection. For example, if you were to move your Web site from one Web hosting service to another, you would need to edit the connection to point to the new hosting service. You might also need to modify the connection if your organization began using a staging server; in that case, you would edit the connection to point to the staging server instead of the production server.

To edit a site connection:

1. Choose Edit > My Connections (Contribute > My Connections). The My Connections window appears.

2. Select the connection you want to edit, then click Edit.

3. The Connection Wizard opens. Use the Wizard to make any changes to the connection. If you need more information about using the Connection Wizard, see "Using the Connection Wizard," earlier in this chapter.

✔ Tips

- You can't duplicate an existing connection as a basis for a new connection. You must create the new connection from scratch.

- If you connect to the site using a connection key sent to you by your network administrator, the site connection information will be locked and you will only be able to change your user information. These sites will be identified in the My Connection dialogs with a globe and key icon as described in the "Connection Icons" sidebar.

Connection Icons

A close examination of the different connections in the My Connections window shows an icon next to the name of each Web site (**Figure 2.30**). Each of these icons tells you something different about the kind of connection:

- The icon with a computer and globe shows that the connection was created with the Connection Wizard.

- The icon overlaid with a key shows that the connection was created with a connection key.

- An icon with a slash through it indicates that the connection is disabled.

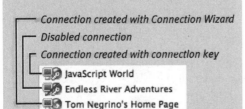

Connection created with Connection Wizard
Disabled connection
Connection created with connection key

JavaScript World
Endless River Adventures
Tom Negrino's Home Page

Figure 2.30 The icons in the My Connections window signify how the connection was created.

Working Offline

Most of the time, you'll want to use Contribute while connected to your Web server, whether that Web server is on the Internet or elsewhere on your local area network. But Contribute also allows you to create new documents and edit existing draft pages when you're not connected to any network. This is called *working offline*.

To work offline:

1. Choose File > Work Offline (Contribute > Work Offline).

   Contribute disconnects from the network.

2. You might now choose to edit any drafts or documents that appear under the Pages section of the sidebar or you can choose File > New Page.

To reconnect to your network:

◆ Click the Work Online button in the Edit bar.

   or

   Uncheck the Work Offline item in the File (Contribute) menu.

Disabling Site Connections

Connection Disabling is a feature that tells Contribute not to pay attention to a site connection. When you disable a connection, Contribute won't let you edit or publish pages on the Web site, though you can still browse the site.

Connections are automatically disabled if a connection is no longer usable (for instance, if there is a network failure or if the Web server becomes unreachable for some other reason). You can also manually disable a network connection by choosing Edit > My Connections (Contribute > My Connections) (**Figure 2.1**), selecting a Web site from the list, and clicking the Disable button.

One of the benefits of disabling a site connection is that Contribute starts up faster, especially if you have connections to several sites. When you launch Contribute, the program connects to all of the enabled Web sites and ensures that its copies of each Web site's templates are identical to the current versions of those templates, as someone else might have updated the templates since the last time you worked on the site. The more enabled site connections you have, the longer the process takes. You can see that it would be beneficial to disable connections for sites you don't need to update very often, or if you're working with a slow network connection, such as a dial-up modem.

The easiest way to reenable a disabled connection is to browse to the site, then click the Retry Connection button on the toolbar.

BUILDING
WEB PAGES

3

Now that you've made one or more site connections, you're ready to take advantage of Macromedia Contribute's ability to Browse, Edit, and Publish pages to your Web sites.

Contribute gives you a wide variety of tools for creating and editing Web pages. You can build new pages from scratch; use the built-in Sample Pages; create new pages based on Macromedia Dreamweaver templates; or even copy existing pages on your Web site. You can also edit existing pages and their properties, and allow your coworkers to review your draft pages before you publish them to the site. If you make a mistake, you can even use Contribute to roll back pages to a previous version. In this chapter, you'll learn how to do all these things and more.

Browsing Sites

Contribute has a built-in Web browser (**Figure 3.1**). On Windows, it's an embedded version of the Microsoft Internet Explorer Web browser. The Mac OS X version uses an integrated version of the Opera browser. You use this built-in browser to navigate to pages you want to edit. You can also use it just as you would most Web browsers, to view HTML pages on the Web or on your local network. The familiar Address bar is there to enter Web addresses, as are the Back and Forward buttons. You navigate to new pages by clicking links, just as in any browser. When your pointer hovers over a link, the link's destination address appears in the browser's status bar at the bottom of the browser window.

You can browse to any Web site with Contribute, but you can only edit pages on Web sites for which you have a connection key (see Chapter 2, "Making a Site Connection," for more information on connection keys). When you browse to a page on a site where you have permission to edit, the Edit Page button is enabled in the toolbar.

Contribute's browser is useful (and essential for working with your sites), but it doesn't always work the same way as a stand-alone browser; see the "Contribute Browser Limitations" sidebar for details. Still, it's easy to use and even has several shortcut keys to speed your browsing (see **Table 3.1**).

Browser toolbar

Edit Page   *Status bar*

Figure 3.1 Contribute's built-in browser allows you to navigate to pages you can then edit.

Table 3.1

Browser Navigation Shortcuts		
SHORTCUT (WINDOWS)	SHORTCUT (MAC)	WHAT IT DOES
Alt-Left Arrow	Opt-Left Arrow	Back; returns to the previously viewed page.
Alt-Right Arrow	Opt-Right Arrow	Forward; displays the page you were viewing before you clicked Back.
Esc	Esc	Stops loading a page.
F5	Cmd-R	Reloads the current page.
Ctrl-O	Cmd-O	Displays the Go to Web Address dialog; equivalent to clicking and typing in the Address field.
Ctrl-Shift-O	Cmd-Shift-O	Displays the Choose File on Website dialog, allowing you to select a file on one of the sites for which you have a connection key. Equivalent to clicking the Choose button on the toolbar.

To browse to any Web page:

1. If necessary, click Browser in the Pages panel.

2. In the Address bar, type the Web address (URL) of the page you want to view.

3. Press Enter (Return).

   Contribute displays the Web page.

✛ Contribute Browser Limitations

Contribute's built-in browser is an embedded version of Internet Explorer (Windows) and Opera 6 (Mac), but it doesn't have all of those browser's capabilities. There are several things Contribute's browser doesn't do, or does in a different fashion than standalone browsers.

◆ Contribute's browser doesn't allow you to open more than one main browser window at a time. If, while browsing, you click a link that is set to open the resulting page in a new window, the new window will open in your computer's default browser (usually Internet Explorer on Windows). On the Mac, you'll get a dialog asking if you want to open the page in your default browser.

◆ Most online shopping carts don't work in Contribute's browser. Use a standalone browser to do your shopping.

◆ The built-in browser also has trouble with many password-protected Web sites. So you probably should use a different browser to do your online banking and pick up your Web-based email.

BROWSING SITES

You can use another method to browse to a page:

1. Choose View > Go to Web Address, or press Ctrl-O (Cmd-O).

   The Go To Web Address dialog appears (**Figure 3.2**).

2. Type the URL of the page you want to view.

3. Click OK.

   Contribute displays the Web page.

✔ Tips

■ There's a bug in Contribute for Windows that requires you to click OK in the Go To Web Address dialog; pressing Enter won't do the trick.

■ You can jump back to the browser at any time by choosing View > Browser, or by pressing Ctrl-Shift-B (Cmd-Shift-B).

■ Bookmarks you create in Contribute for Windows (by choosing Bookmarks > Add Bookmark) also appear in Internet Explorer's Favorites menu, inside a folder called Contribute Bookmarks. Similarly, favorites you create in Internet Explorer for Windows appear in Contribute's Bookmarks menu, under Other Bookmarks. Unfortunately, no similar convenience appears on Macintosh.

■ If a page is taking too long to appear, click the Stop button in the toolbar to stop loading the page.

■ You can reload a page in the browser by clicking the Refresh button in the toolbar.

■ The Windows version of Contribute uses whatever version of Internet Explorer is installed on the computer. Updating Internet Explorer will update Contribute's browser too. Opera 6 is built into the Macintosh version, and cannot be updated by the user.

Figure 3.2 The Go To Web Address dialog presents another way of browsing to a page.

Figure 3.3 Jump quickly between your site connections with the Home Pages pop-up menu in the Browser toolbar.

Figure 3.4 The Choose File on Website dialog is the fastest way to browse to a particular file on one of your sites.

Figure 3.5 The Preview pane in the Choose File on Website dialog tells you if you have found the right file.

Browsing your sites

Contribute offers two tools on the Browser toolbar that help you navigate easily to sites for which you have established connections. The first tool is the Home Pages pop-up menu, and the second tool is the Choose button.

The Home Pages pop-up menu (**Figure 3.3**) contains a list of all the home pages for the Web sites you can edit. It's like a list of favorites that allows you to move rapidly among your Web sites.

The Choose button allows you to quickly find and browse to a particular file on one of your Web sites. Clicking Choose when you're not already displaying one of your sites brings up the Choose File on Website dialog, with all your sites listed (**Figure 3.4**). If you know the file name and it's location, it's very easy to find any file on any of your Web sites this way, much faster than typing URLs in the Address bar, because you can navigate directly through folders to pick files. If you're already browsing one of the Web sites you can edit, clicking the Choose button brings up the Choose File on Website dialog already set to browse the files on that Web site. The Preview pane of the dialog helps you find things fast (**Figure 3.5**).

✔ Tips

■ The names of the menu items in the Home Pages pop-up menu are taken from the names of the Web sites in the My Connections dialog. You can edit the names in that dialog to make the menu items shorter or more descriptive.

■ You can also open the Choose File on Website dialog by pressing Ctrl-Shift-O (Cmd-Shift-O).

■ The items at the top of the Choose File on Website dialog can help you with navigation and file management (**Figure 3.6**). The "Look in" pop-up menu allows you to move quickly among your different Web sites. If you've been digging deep into a site, the Up One Level button makes it easy to move up to the next level in the folder hierarchy. Using the New Folder and Delete Folder buttons, you can change your site's folder structure.

Figure 3.6 You can accomplish some useful navigation and file management with the controls at the top of the Choose File on Website dialog.

Figure 3.7 When you're creating a new page using the New Page dialog, Contribute automatically selects the Blank Web Page for you.

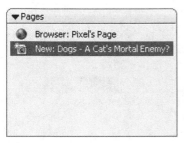

Figure 3.8 New pages are listed in the Pages panel of the sidebar.

Creating New Pages

Most of the time when you're working with Contribute, you create new pages based on template pages—either the example pages that come with Contribute or templates created for you by your site's designers in Dreamweaver or other Web design and development tools. Creating new pages from templates is discussed later in this chapter.

Alternatively, you can create the page and create a link to the new page in one operation. In fact, that's how Macromedia recommends you create pages, so as to avoid orphan pages—pages with no link to them—on your Web site. See "Creating New Pages from Links" in Chapter 6 for more information.

Sometimes, though, you simply want to create a new blank page in one of your existing Web sites, and Contribute can do that, too.

To create a new blank page:

1. Browse to the Web site where you want to add a new page. It must be a site for which you have established a connection.

2. Click New Page on the toolbar.

   or

   Choose File > New Page, or press Crtl-N (Cmd-N).

   The New Page dialog appears. In this dialog, all your Web sites will be listed, but the site in which you're working will be expanded and Blank Web Page will be selected (**Figure 3.7**).

3. Press Tab to highlight the "Page title" box, and enter a title for your new Web page.

   This title will appear as the page's title in Web browsers.

4. Click OK.

   Contribute creates the new page and lists it as a new page in the Pages panel (**Figure 3.8**). You may now add content to the page.

continues on next page

CREATING NEW PAGES

5. Click Publish to save the new page to your server.

If you haven't linked the new page to any other page, Contribute displays a warning dialog (**Figure 3.9**).

6. Click Yes or No. Remember, if you publish the page, you need to create a link to it if you want site visitors to find it.

7. Contribute displays the Publish New Page dialog, where you need to enter the filename for the new page (**Figure 3.10**).

The filename will appear at the end of the Web address for the page. By default, Contribute enters the filename as the page title with spaces removed and the file-name extension .htm appended. If desired, enter your changes to the filename.

8. (Optional) If you want to save the new page in a folder on your Web site other than the current folder (which is the folder that contains the current page that is displayed in the browser). Click the Choose Folder button to open the Choose Folder dialog. Navigate to where you want to save the new page, and click the Select button. The dialog will show the URL of the new page you are creating.

The Publish New Page dialog reappears.

9. Click Publish.

Contribute publishes your new page to the Web site and displays a congratulatory dialog (**Figure 3.11**).

Contribute switches back to its browser and displays the newly published page.

✔ Tips

■ Contribute considers a page to be a new page until you publish it to the server, even if you click the Save for Later button.

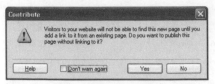

Figure 3.9 Contribute reminds you that if you don't create a link to the page you've created, visitors won't be able to find it.

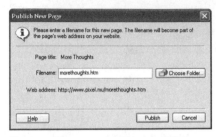

Figure 3.10 You can accept the default filename Contribute gives you, but it's usually better to edit the filename so that it is all lowercase.

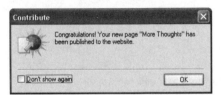

Figure 3.11 Contribute congratulates you on publishing your page.

■ The default filename Contribute provides in the Publish New Page dialog often has both upper- and lowercase text. It's better to manually change it to all lowercase; otherwise, your site's visitors will need to type in the exact filename in order to get to your page.

■ Many alert dialogs in Contribute have a "Don't show again" check box. Once you get used to using Contribute, you might want to select these check boxes to speed your work.

■ Contribute doesn't like pages without titles; it won't let you create a new page until you give it a page title.

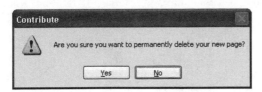

Figure 3.12 Are you sure you want to delete that page?

Canceling pages

When you're editing a new page that you created, you can discard the new page by canceling it. If you're editing a draft of an existing page, canceling the draft page discards your changes and keeps the currently published version of the page.

To cancel a new or draft page:

1. In the Pages panel, select the new or draft page you want to cancel.

    Contribute displays the page in the browser window.

2. Click Cancel on the toolbar.

    or

    Choose File > Cancel Draft.

3. Click Yes when Contribute asks if you want to permanently delete your new page (**Figure 3.12**).

Deleting pages

You can delete Web pages or any kind of file from your Web site as long as your site administrator has given you file-deleting permissions as part of your connection key.

To delete a file from your Web site:

1. Browse to the page or file you want to delete.

2. Choose File > Delete Page.

    The menu item will be disabled if you don't have permission to delete pages on your Web site or if you have an unpublished draft of the page.

    Contribute displays an alert box asking if you're sure you want to delete.

3. Click Yes to confirm the deletion.

CREATING NEW PAGES

Building New Pages from Sample Pages

Contribute comes with 14 built-in sample Web pages you can use as templates for your own Web pages. You have a choice of three colors for most of the sample pages: Silver (the page elements are shades of a light gray), Forest (medium green shades), and Sky (darker blues), as listed in **Table 3.2**.

These sample templates make a good starting point for many pages. They aren't especially fancy, but they can help you get the job done quickly and will be all that some people need to whip out a page on deadline. The pre-built calendar templates are especially useful.

Figure 3.13 Contribute's Sample Web Pages are a quick way to get started building pages.

To create new pages from sample pages:

1. Browse to the Web site where you want to add a new page. It must be a site for which you have established a connection.

2. Click New Page on the toolbar.

   or

   Choose File > New Page, or press Ctrl-N (Cmd-N).

3. In the New Page dialog, click the small plus button (on the Mac, the small disclosure triangle) next to Sample Web Pages.

   The four folders for the page categories—Business, Collaboration, Personal, and Calendars—appear.

4. Click the small plus button next to one of the categories to disclose its contents.

5. Select one of the Sample Web Pages to view it in the Preview pane (**Figure 3.13**).

   Below the preview is a short description of the template.

Table 3.2

CATEGORY	TEMPLATE NAME	COLORS
Contribute's Sample Pages		
Business	General Content	Silver
	Two-Column	Forest
	Grouped Item List	Sky
	Home Page	
	Table Data	
Personal	Photo Album Page	Silver
	Résumé	Forest
	Multiple-Photo Album Page	Sky
Calendars	Generic Month	Silver
	Individual August 2003 through December 2005 calendars	
Collaboration	Project Home Page	Silver
	Meeting Notes	Forest
	Presentation Slide Report	Sky

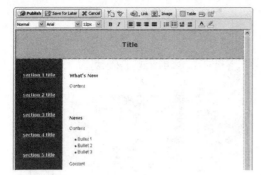

Figure 3.14 Sample Web Pages aren't especially pretty, but they are convenient.

6. Press Tab to highlight the "Page title" box, and enter a title for your new Web page.

7. Click OK.

Contribute creates the new page based on the template (**Figure 3.14**).

✔ Tips

■ Because of a bug in Contribute for Windows, you can't double-click folders in the New Page dialog to disclose their contents. Click the small plus buttons next to folders instead. There's no such problem on Macintosh.

■ You can make your own Sample Pages and add them to the New Page dialog; see "Creating Sample Pages Templates," in Chapter 8 for details.

■ As with any page you create in Contribute, it's a good idea to create the new page and the link to the page at the same time.

Building New Pages from Dreamweaver Templates

Chances are, many of the pages you'll create as a content contributor will be based on templates created in Macromedia Dreamweaver MX. These templates will be created by your site's designer and will be made available to you by your site's administrator.

A Dreamweaver template can contain two types of regions. *Contribute users cannot modify locked regions.* Examples of locked regions on a template might be navigation bars, some page backgrounds, and section titles. *Editable regions* are containers for content, which could include text or images, that can be changed by the Contribute user. Contribute shows you the editable regions on draft pages, outlined in green, with tabs for the names of each region (**Figure 3.15**).

This section of the book merely shows you the basics of creating pages from Dreamweaver templates. For more information, see Chapter 8, "Using Dreamweaver Templates."

To create pages from Dreamweaver templates:

1. Browse to the Web site where you want to add a new page. It must be a Web site for which you have established a connection.

2. Click New Page on the toolbar.
   or
   Choose File > New Page, or press Ctrl-N (Cmd-N).

Locked regions

Editable regions

Figure 3.15 In this Dreamweaver template, the editable regions are shown outlined in green, with tabs for the name of each region.

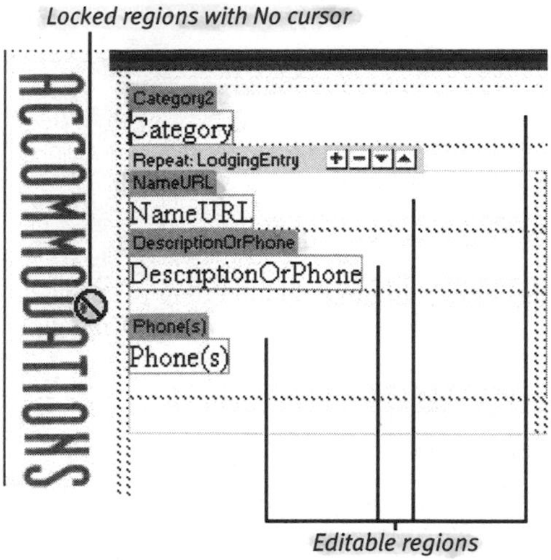

Locked regions with No cursor

Editable regions

Figure 3.16 The No cursor tells you where you can't edit.

3. In the New Page dialog, click the small plus button (disclosure triangle) next to Templates.

The templates defined for your Web site appear.

4. Select a template to display it in the Preview pane.

5. Press Tab to highlight the "Page title" box, and enter a title for your new Web page.

6. Click OK.

Contribute creates the new page based on the template.

✔ Tips

■ Your Web site administrator can designate any page on your site as a template, which will then be available in the Templates category in the New Page dialog. See Chapter 8, "Assigning Permissions," for more details.

■ The cursor turns into the international symbol for "no" (a circle with a diagonal slash through it) when you enter locked regions in Dreamweaver templates, indicating that you don't have permission to edit (**Figure 3.16**).

Copying Existing Pages

Most of the time you'll want to use templates with Contribute, but sometimes you may want to duplicate a lot of an existing page's content, and a simple copy with a few changes will do.

When you create a copy of a page, you must first create a new page, and subsequently make a link to it. Unlike most situations in Contribute where you create pages, here you cannot create a copy and add a link to it at the same time.

To make a copy of an existing page:

1. Browse to the page you want to copy.

2. Click New Page on the toolbar.

   or

   Choose File > New Page, or press Ctrl-N (Cmd-N).

3. In the New Page dialog, click Copy of Current Page.

   The Preview pane shows you what the copy will look like.

4. Press Tab to highlight the "Page title" box, and enter a title for the new page.

5. Click OK.

   Contribute creates a new page that is a copy of the page you were browsing, and then enters Edit mode.

✔ Tips

- You cannot create a copy of a page that contains a frameset.

- You can only copy pages you're viewing with the Contribute browser; you can't make a copy of a draft page.

- Unfortunately, you can't copy a page from one of your Web sites to another Web site.

Editing Existing Pages

By now, editing pages on your Web sites should be pretty clear. First you use the Contribute browser to view a page on a site you have permission to edit, then you enter Editing mode.

To edit pages in Contribute:

1. Browse to the page you want to edit.

   Use the Choose button in the browser toolbar to navigate to pages quickly.

2. Click the Edit Page button in the toolbar.

   or

   Choose File > Edit Page, or press Ctrl-Shift-E (Cmd-Shift-E).

   The draft page appears in the editor, and the draft's title appears in the Pages panel in the sidebar.

3. Edit the page.

4. Click Publish to save your work and publish it on your Website.

✔ Tips

- You'll usually be connected to your Web site when using Contribute, but you can create new draft pages or continue editing existing draft pages (usually pages you created while working online) in Contribute's Offline mode. Choose File > Work Offline. Offline mode is especially useful if you're using a slow network connection, like a dial-up modem, or if you are not connected to the Internet at all.

- Sometimes Contribute displays a message saying you can't edit a page because someone else is editing the page. If this happens, you might have to wait until the other person is finished with the page, or you can contact your site administrator.

Setting Page Properties

Page properties are settings that affect the entire page you're editing. They include the page title, background image or color, margins, default text color, and link colors.

✛ You can change the page properties for any page you can edit unless the page is based on a template or you have been restricted to text-only editing by your site administrator. In those cases, you're only allowed to change the page title, and most of the options in the Page Properties dialog will be inactive.

To set page properties:

1. Browse to the page for which you want to set page properties, and then click Edit Page in the toolbar.

   Contribute creates a draft of the page.

2. Click the Page Properties button in the toolbar (**Figure 3.17**).

   or

   Choose Format > Page Properties, or press Ctrl-J (Cmd-J).

   The Page Properties dialog appears (**Figure 3.18**).

3. Change the page title. The title you give your page will be displayed in the Web browser's title bar.

   or

   Change the page's background: Click the Browse button next to the "Background image." box. A menu pops up with two choices: Images on My Computer and Images on Website. Choose one of these locations to navigate to a graphic file you want to use as a background for the page.

   or

Page Properties

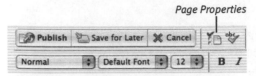

Figure 3.17 Use the Page Properties button on the toolbar to change page attributes.

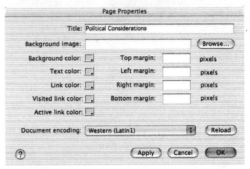

Figure 3.18 The Page Properties dialog allows you to edit the page's title, change the background color or image, and much more.

Color box

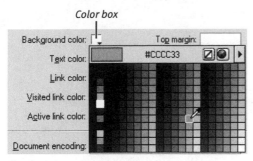

Figure 3.19 Use the color picker to change the background, text, or link color.

Choose a link color: Click one of the color boxes. The color picker appears (**Figure 3.19**). Click on a color with the eyedropper to select it; the color can be any color in the picker or on your desktop. See the "Pick Your Link Color" sidebar for details.

or

Change the page's margins: Enter a value, in pixels, for one or more of the four margins of the page. Leaving a value blank is the same as entering zero.

or

Change document encoding for a non-Latin alphabet: From the "Document encoding" drop-down menu, select the character set for the page. You use this only when you'll be adding content in a language that uses a non-Western (non-Latin) alphabet. The default document encoding, Western (Latin1), is appropriate for English and Western European languages. Encodings are also available for Japanese, Chinese, Korean, Central European languages, Cyrillic, Greek, Icelandic, and Other. By setting the correct document encoding, you ensure that Web browsers can display the proper set of fonts to view your page.

4. Click OK to accept your changes.

✔ Tips

- Most of the time, a background image and a background color are mutually exclusive. If you select a background image for the page, your site's visitors won't see the background color.

- Use background images with care and delicacy. Chances are, you've seen pages where the background image obscured the content, making the text all but unreadable. Use subtle images.

- If you select a text color, it will be the default color for text on the page. That doesn't mean you can't change the color of selected text on the page. See Chapter 4, "Editing Page Content," for more information.

- Templates created in Dreamweaver maintain their document encoding when used in Contribute, so if you often need to create pages in non-Western languages, ask your site designer to build a Dreamweaver template with the correct encoding.

- On Windows, you can close the color picker by pressing Esc.

SETTING PAGE PROPERTIES

Pick Your Link Color

You can set colors for three kinds of links in Contribute: Link, Visited Link, and Active Link.

The **Link color** is the link's initial color before a user clicks the link. The default link color for most browsers is blue.

The **Visited Link color** is the color to which a link changes after a user has clicked the link and visited its destination page. For most browsers, the default color for visited links is purple.

The **Active Link color** is the color a link turns if a user holds down the mouse button after clicking the link. The standard default color for active links is red.

You can set alternative colors for any of these, but be aware that if you change them, it may be a bit harder for some users to navigate your site, because links may not appear as they expect. It's also not a good idea to set the same color for Link and Visited Link, because users won't be able to tell what parts of your site they've already visited.

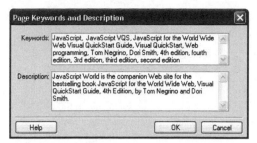

Figure 3.20 Page keywords and descriptions help search engines find your site.

Setting Page Keywords and Descriptions

Page keywords and descriptions are bits of information that your site's visitors never see but are read by browsers and Internet search engines. Search engines use keywords to improve the accuracy of their search results. Some search engines also use descriptions to display the results.

Page keywords and descriptions are two types of special HTML tags called *META tags*. Meta information is information about information; in this case, the keywords and page description are bits of information about the page itself.

To set page keywords and descriptions:

1. Browse to the page where you want to set keywords or descriptions, and then click Edit Page in the toolbar.

    Contribute creates a draft of the page.

2. Choose Format > Keywords and Description, or press Ctrl-Alt-K (Cmd-Opt-K).

    The Page Keywords and Description dialog appears (**Figure 3.20**).

3. Enter your keywords in the Keywords field.

    Keywords in this field are separated by commas. You should try to use keywords you believe people would use when trying to find your site in an Internet search engine such as Google, MSN Search, or Yahoo! Search.

4. Enter your page description in the Description field.

5. Click OK to save your keywords and descriptions.

6. Click Publish to save your work to the server.

✔ Tip

- If you want to see your keywords and descriptions, you need to open the page in an external browser such as Internet Explorer or Safari, and then view the page's source code. See "Previewing Pages in External Browsers," later in this chapter, for more information.

Editing Framed Pages

A Web page with *frames* is split into two or more rectangular areas, each of which has independent content. Frames are commonly used to define navigation and content areas for a page. The frame with the navigation area remains constant, and the content area changes when the user clicks a link in the navigation area. For example, many online shopping sites use frames to display their products in the content frame while allowing the user to browse to new content using the navigation frame. Frames can scroll independently, and the Web designer can even turn off scroll bars for particular frames.

When a user views a Web page that has been created with two frames, the browser is actually using three different files to display the page. In addition to the two frames the user sees, there's a third page, the *frameset* page. The frameset page is an HTML page that is invisible to the user but tells the browser how to display the frames and the pages they contain. It stores information about the size, location, and layout of each frame. Each frame within the frameset is a separate HTML file.

Contribute doesn't allow you to create or edit framesets, which must be created or changed in Dreamweaver or some other Web design tool, but it does allow you to edit any of the HTML pages within the frameset. In other words, you can change the content of any of the frames. Contribute does this by opening the HTML page that makes up the frame as a draft page.

When you browse to a page that has frames, the individual pages that make up the frames can come from the same or even different Web sites. You can edit content in any frame in which you have permission to edit.

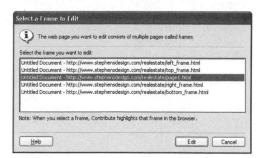

Figure 3.21 Choose the frame you want to edit.

Framed border   Selected frame

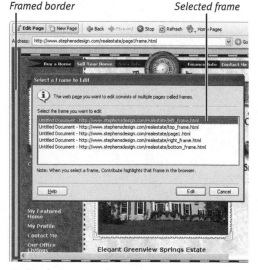

Figure 3.22 Selecting a frame in the Select a Frame to Edit dialog puts a border around that frame in the editing window.

To edit content in a frame:

1. Browse to the page with the frames you want to edit.

2. Click the Edit Page button.

   Contribute displays the Select a Frame to Edit dialog (**Figure 3.21**). This dialog contains a list of all the frames that make up the page (but does not include the frameset page). The list includes the page titles and URLs for each of the frame pages.

3. In the dialog, select the frame you want to edit.

   Contribute puts a thick red border around the frame you selected, which helps you confirm that you have chosen the correct frame (**Figure 3.22**).

4. Click Edit.

   Contribute opens up the frame page as a new draft page, without the other frames.

5. Make your edits.

6. Click the Publish button to save your changes to the server.

✔ Tips

- If any of the frames in the frameset have been marked by the page designer as noneditable areas, these frames will appear in gray text in the Select a Frame to Edit dialog, and won't be selectable.

- Normally, when you have a draft page open, and you switch back to the browser and view the published version of the page, Contribute shows, in its message area directly below the Browser toolbar, that you have an unpublished draft of the page you are viewing. For some reason, Contribute doesn't do that when you have a draft of framed page.

Saving Page Drafts

One of the nice things about Contribute is that although you can save draft pages manually, you'll hardly ever need to. Contribute saves your work automatically in the following situations:

◆ When you switch to the browser

◆ When you switch to another draft page

◆ When you publish the current draft page

◆ When you choose File > Publish As New Page

◆ When you exit Contribute

If you want to save draft pages manually, you can do so by choosing File > Save, or by pressing Ctrl-S (Cmd-S).

✔ Tip

■ Contribute performs most of its automatic saving when you switch from one page to another. Therefore, it's probably not a bad idea to hit Ctrl-S (Cmd-S) from time to time when you create a large amount of content for a particular page in Contribute, just to make sure your work is preserved in the (let's hope unlikely) event that the system or Contribute crashes.

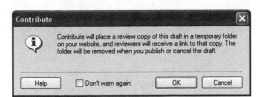

Figure 3.23 When you send a page for review by email, Contribute apprises you of the process.

Letting Coworkers Review Your Pages

It's fairly common to have your boss or other coworkers review your draft pages before you publish them on your Web site. Contribute allows you to notify coworkers via email when a draft page is waiting for their review. One of the beauties of this review process is that recipients don't have to have Contribute, or Dreamweaver, or any other Web design tool; all they need is a Web browser and the ability to receive email.

When you make a draft available for review, Contribute does two things:

◆ It creates a temporary copy of the draft page on the same server where you publish your Web site. This temporary copy can't be edited by the reviewer.

◆ It creates an email message in your default email application that contains a Web address pointing to the temporary copy of the draft page.

After viewing the temporary copy of your draft page, the reviewer should send you his or her feedback in an email. You can then make changes to the draft page in Contribute. After that, you can either send the changed draft for additional review (repeating the review process) or simply publish the draft page.

To send a draft page for review:

1. In the Pages panel of the sidebar, select the draft you want to send for review.

   The draft page appears in the editing pane.

2. Choose File > Email Review.

   Contribute displays a dialog that describes the review process (**Figure 3.23**).

continues on the next page

LETTING COWORKERS REVIEW YOUR PAGES

3. Click OK.

Contribute takes a moment to create the temporary copy of the draft page on the server, then launches your email application and creates a new message (**Figure 3.24**). The new message has a subject automatically inserted, and the body of the message contains a link to the temporary copy of the draft page.

4. Address and send the email message.

After the mail has been sent, Contribute uses the message area below the toolbar to inform you that you posted the draft for review, with the date and time (**Figure 3.25**). There is also a link that allows you to view the draft version you sent for review.

✔ Tips

- If the page being reviewed is part of a frameset, the review address is for the single page you edited, not the entire frameset.

- When you publish or cancel the draft you sent for review, Contribute deletes the temporary copy of the draft it placed on the server for the reviewer.

- If for some reason Contribute cannot open your email application, you can still create the email message by clicking the Click Here link in the message area under the toolbar. The temporary copy of the draft page appears in the browser. Copy the URL for the temporary page from the browser's Address bar, and paste the address into an email message.

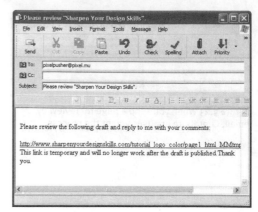

Figure 3.24 The page-review announcement email in Outlook Express for Windows.

Figure 3.25 After you send a page for review, Contribute reminds you in the message area below the toolbar.

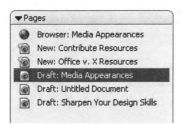

Figure 3.26 The two new pages will be published when the selected draft page is published, because the draft page contains links to both the new pages.

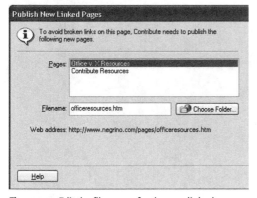

Figure 3.27 Edit the filenames for the new linked pages.

Publishing Your Pages

When you've finished editing a draft, you're ready to publish it to your Web site for the world to see. If you are publishing an update to an existing page, Contribute replaces the current version of the page that is live on your Web site with the new version.

Because it is possible for you to create links to new, previously unpublished pages as you work on a draft page, Contribute also publishes those new pages when you publish the current draft page; otherwise, you would have a page on your Web site with links to nowhere (**Figure 3.26**).

To publish page updates:

1. In the Pages panel of the sidebar, select the draft you want to publish.

2. Click Publish.

   If the draft page doesn't have links to any new pages, Contribute simply publishes the draft to your Web server. But if the draft contains links to any new pages, the Publish New Linked Pages dialog appears (**Figure 3.27**).

3. For each of the new pages, edit the filename and choose the folder where you want the page to reside on your server.

   Note that Contribute displays the Web address for each of the new pages.

4. Click Publish All.

✔ Tip

■ The default filename that Contribute provides in the Publish New Linked Pages dialog usually contains both upper- and lowercase text. Change the name to all lowercase to make it easier for site visitors to type the page's URL and easily reach your site.

Publishing existing pages as new pages

The equivalent of Save As in Contribute is its ability to make changes to an existing page and then publish it as a new page. Unlike simply publishing a draft, publishing an existing page as a new page doesn't overwrite the existing page.

To publish an existing page as a new page:

1. Browse to an existing page on your Web site.

2. Click Edit Page.

   Contribute creates a draft of the page.

3. Make your changes to the draft.

4. Choose File > Publish as New Page.

   The Publish As New Page dialog appears (**Figure 3.28**). If you haven't linked the new page from an existing page, Contribute displays a warning. After you publish the new page, you should create a link to it from one of the other existing pages on your Web site.

5. Change the page title and the filename for the new page.

   If you don't change the filename, Contribute automatically changes it for you so that you don't accidentally overwrite the existing page when you publish it.

6. Click Publish.

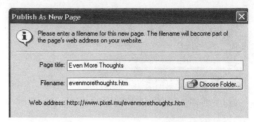

Figure 3.28 When you publish an existing page as a new page, you'll need to edit the filename for the new page in the Publish As New Page dialog.

Figure 3.29 You can roll back a page to any previous version, up to the limit the site administrator set for you (in this case, that limit was three versions).

Rolling Back to Previous Page Versions

Contribute has the ability to *roll back* published pages—that is, revert to previously published versions of the pages. Think of it as a sort of "Super Undo" for your Web sites. You can roll back to the last published version, or to any saved version.

Contribute can roll back to "only" 99 versions of a given page, but your site administrator will probably limit you to far fewer rollbacks.

To roll back to a previous page version:

1. Browse to the page you want to roll back.

2. Choose File > Roll Back to Previous Version. Contribute gets the version information from the server and displays the Roll Back Page dialog (**Figure 3.29**).

3. From the list of page versions at the top of the dialog, choose a previous version. Contribute displays the page in the Preview section. If it's not the version you want, select another.

4. Click Roll Back. Contribute replaces the currently published version of the page with the previously published version.

✔ Tips

■ When you roll back a current version of a page to a previously published version, the current version is saved on the server as a rollback version, and you can revert back to it.

■ Site administrators can enable or disable rollback for groups of users. See Chapter Pg. 195→10, "Site Administration," for more details.

■ As long as you have the ability to edit a page, you can roll it back. Contribute doesn't restrict rollbacks to the person who last edited or published the page.

■ The Roll Back Page dialog is resizable, so you can preview more of the rollback version.

Printing Pages

Now that we have all reached the nirvana of the paperless office, there's never any need to print pages. All right, I admit I'm dreaming. You might want to print your pages for review by people who aren't online, for the boss who never quite got the hang of this newfangled Web thing, or simply because sometimes you can see errors on paper faster than you can see them on-screen. Contribute allows you to do a print preview before you print a page.

To preview and print a page:

1. Browse to the page you want to print.

2. (Windows) Choose File > Print Preview.

   or

   (Macintosh) Choose File > Print, then click the Preview button in the Print dialog.

   The page appears in the preview window (**Figure 3.30**). You can change the page's magnification to get a closer look.

3. Click Print.

✔ Tip

■ In Windows, if you don't want to preview a page first, you can simply choose File > Print.

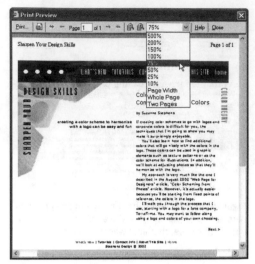

Figure 3.30 You can view a page at several different magnifications in the Page Preview dialog. This is the Windows version.

EDITING
PAGE CONTENT

Macromedia Contribute is all about making it easier to edit the content of Web pages, and the program provides a wide selection of tools to help you create and style your content. Most of these tools will be familiar to you, as they work in ways that are reminiscent of other tools you use, such as word processors. That's no accident: Macromedia made the editing experience as familiar as possible so that users with little or no experience building Web pages could get started quickly with Contribute.

In this chapter, you'll learn how to edit and style text on Web pages, organize your text for easier reading, and check the spelling of your documents before you publish them for all to see.

Basic Text Editing

Like most word-processing and desktop publishing applications, Contribute respects the usual conventions for text entry. You can use the arrow keys, backspace key, Page Up key, Page Down key, and other keys to move around the draft window. As you type, text wraps from line to line. You can cut and paste text, or use drag and drop to move text around. You can also drag text from another application, such as Microsoft Word, into the Contribute draft window.

That's the Breaks

Paragraph breaks in Web page editors have traditionally used the HTML <p> tag, which Web browsers display by inserting a blank line between paragraphs that use the <p> tag. This is perfectly workable—after all, that's how most Web pages have worked for years—but it doesn't offer the Web page designer much in the way of typographical control. That control arrived with the advent of Cascading Style Sheets (CSS), an extension to HTML that allows designers to precisely control the formatting and positioning of text. Being a modern Web tool, Contribute understands CSS, and the site administrator can set a user permission that makes Contribute use CSS styles instead of the HTML <p> tag for paragraph breaks. With CSS styles, pressing Enter (Return) creates a paragraph break without inserting a blank line between paragraphs, so that Contribute works more like a standard word processor (**Figure 4.1**).

Despite our initially limited broadcast day, it makes sense to build the facility with the broadcast capability to handle our ultimate projected requirements of three full-time channels. It is usually more expensive to add on broadcast capability.
The facility should be designed to take maximum advantage of automation, so that we can get the most out of our scarce people resources. Better automation will cost more upfront, but will allow us to get the job done with less employee burnout and an operational cost savings.

Despite our initially limited broadcast day, it makes sense to build the facility with the broadcast capability to handle our ultimate projected requirements of three full-time channels. It is usually more expensive to add on broadcast capability.

The facility should be designed to take maximum advantage of automation, so that we can get the most out of our scarce people resources. Better automation will cost more upfront, but will allow us to get the job done with less employee burnout and an operational cost savings.

Figure 4.1 Paragraph breaks using CSS (top) look more natural than paragraph breaks created with HTML tags (bottom).

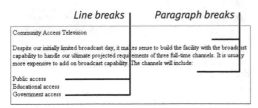

Figure 4.2 A paragraph break produces white space above and below the paragraph. Line breaks do not.

To type text into a draft:

1. Browse to the page you want to edit, then click Edit Page to open the page as a draft.

2. Click in the draft window to place the insertion point where you want it, then just start typing your text. If Contribute inserts a blank line when you press Enter (Return) to make a paragraph break, you can press Shift-Enter (Shift-Return) to make a line break that will not include a blank line (**Figure 4.2**).

To copy and paste text into a draft:

1. Select text from a Web page in the browser, another draft page, or another application.

2. Choose Edit > Copy or press Ctrl-C (Cmd-C).

3. Click in your Contribute draft to place the insertion point, then choose Edit > Paste, or press Ctrl-V (Cmd-V).

✔ Tips

- If you want to paste plain text into Contribute, removing any formatting it had, paste the text by choosing Edit > Paste Text Only, or by pressing Ctrl-Shift-V (Cmd-Shift-V).

- When you have text selected, most of the time you can right-click to cut or copy the text using a shortcut menu. You can also right-click to paste text from the shortcut menu. If you have a single-button mouse on Macintosh, you can Ctrl-click to bring up the shortcut menu.

- Contribute offers Undo and Redo commands in the Edit menu, which can often be very useful in fixing mistakes or repeating operations. You can also use the keyboard shortcuts Ctrl-Z (Cmd-Z) for Undo and Ctrl-Y (Cmd-Y) for Redo.

Using HTML Styles

HTML provides quite a few methods for styling and formatting text that allow Web browsers to display text as bold, italic, colored, and so on.

Contribute shields you from the mechanics of HTML; you don't need to know HTML to add formatting to your draft pages. Like word processors, Contribute uses familiar formatting tools, which you can find in the Editing toolbar (**Figure 4.3**) and in the Format and Insert menus.

Setting font styles

The most common text formatting is to make text bold or italicized, change the font, or change the size. Contribute groups controls for these settings together on the Editing toolbar (**Figure 4.4**). Contribute can also format text as Strikethrough (text with a thin line through it), Emphasis (another style of italic text), Strong (another style of bold text), or Fixed Width (text is monospaced, like old-fashioned typewriter type, or as in the Courier font).

Your site administrator can allow or deny users the ability to apply HTML styles, so if some of these controls are disabled, you should check with the administrator.

Figure 4.3 The Editing toolbar provides most of the tools you'll need to change the content on your draft pages.

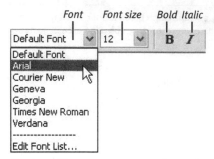

Figure 4.4 The most common text-formatting controls are grouped together on the toolbar.

To make text bold, italic, or underlined:

1. Select the text you want to modify.

2. Click the Bold button on the Editing toolbar, choose Format > Bold, or press Ctrl-B (Cmd-B).

or

Click the Italic button on the Editing toolbar, Choose Format > Italic, or press Ctrl-I (Cmd-I).

or

Choose Format > Underline, or press Ctrl-U (Cmd-U).

The text's appearance changes.

✔ Tips

■ Though you can underline text with Contribute, I don't recommend it, because people have come to expect that underlined text on Web sites indicates a link.

■ To remove a text style, select the text and click the style button again, reselect the menu command, or repeat the shortcut key command. Reapplying the format acts as a toggle, each click turns the formatting on or off.

To format text as Strikethrough, Emphasis, Strong, or Fixed Width:

1. Select the text you want to modify.

2. Choose Format > Other, then pick one of the four choices from the submenu.

✔ Tip

■ Your site administrator may have configured Contribute to use the Strong tag `<strong>` for bold text and the Emphasis tag `<em>` for italic text. These tags tell Contribute to use a more accessible version of the HTML it is creating behind the scenes, helping the visually disabled. You probably won't notice a difference.

USING HTML STYLES

69

Setting fonts and font sizes

In Contribute, you have the ability to set the typeface, or font, for any text on your page. But not all computers or Web browsers use the same fonts. If you specify a font that your site visitor doesn't have on his or her computer, chances are the content won't look the way you intend. Because neither you nor Contribute can be sure what fonts will be available to your site visitors, Contribute uses *font combinations* to work around the problem. Font combinations allow you to provide options for the browser by creating multiple font choices. For example, a font combination could include Arial, Helvetica, and Geneva fonts, and the Web browser would render the page using the first choice available to the browser. If none of the fonts in the combination are installed, the browser will display the text using whatever font is set as the default in the browser's preferences. Contribute comes with six predetermined font combinations, and you can add more as you need them. Each choice in the Font menu represents the first font in that font combination.

Although Contribute is reminiscent of a word processor, it's really not one, and it has the font-size limitations that HTML imposes. In HTML, there are seven standard sizes for fonts, so it's no surprise that there are also seven size choices in Contribute's Font Size menu. In HTML, these sizes are numbered from 1 to 7; Contribute lists them as their roughly equivalent point sizes, from 8 to 36 (**Figure 4.5**). Contribute doesn't give you the freedom to set custom font sizes, though designers, using CSS styles, can set custom sizes in Macromedia Dreamweaver templates (see the section "Using CSS Styles," in this chapter).

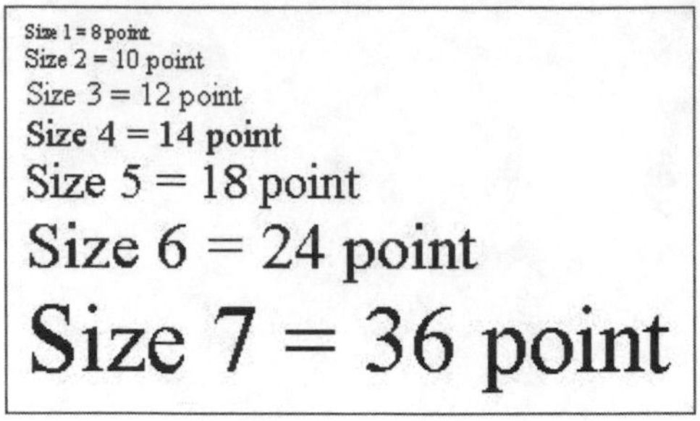

Figure 4.5 The standard HTML font sizes and their Contribute equivalents from the Font Size menu.

The subject of font sizes on Web pages is actually quite complex, and it has generated much gnashing of teeth and heartache between designers, Web browser makers, and standards bodies. But Contribute makes a valiant attempt—largely successful—to shield you from the furor, so we'll leave the angst to others and get on with building our pages.

To set a font or font size:

1. Select the text you want to modify.

2. Choose a different font from the Font menu in the toolbar, or choose Format > Font, and then choose the font from the submenu.

   or

   Choose a different size from the Font Size menu in the toolbar, or choose Format > Size, and then choose the font size from the submenu.

   The text changes appearance.

✔ Tips

■ Contribute's preset font combinations include fonts that are found on nearly every computer sold in the last several years. Most of these fonts are available for both Windows and Macintosh. For example, Arial, Courier, Georgia, Helvetica, Times New Roman, Verdana, and Trebuchet are all fonts that come standard on both platforms.

■ Contribute doesn't allow you to enter a custom font size, as you can in many word processors.

Changing font combinations

You can modify the preset font combinations, and you can also create new font combinations.

To edit the Font List:

1. In the Pages panel of the sidebar, switch to a new or draft page.

   or

   Browse to a page you want to edit, then click Edit Page.

2. Choose Format > Font > Edit Font List.

   The Edit Font List dialog appears (**Figure 4.6**).

3. To add a font combination, click the plus button, then click the arrow buttons in the Available Fonts list and select fonts to move them to the Chosen Fonts list.

   or

   Select a font combination in the Font List, and click the minus button to remove it.

   or

   Use the arrow buttons above the Font List to move a selected font combination up or down in the list.

4. Click OK to save your changes.

✔ Tip

- You can type the name of a font not on your system in the field below the Available Fonts list, then click the left-facing arrow button to add that font to the Chosen Fonts list. You might choose to add a font when you want to use one you know is available on the systems of users who will be visiting your site. For example, if your site will attract many Mac OS X visitors, you can use some of the OS X system fonts, such as Lucida Grande, that are common on the Mac but not on Windows.

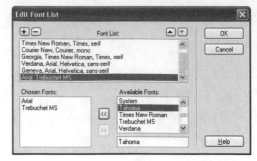

Figure 4.6 The Edit Font List dialog lets you define new font combinations.

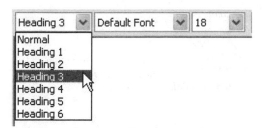

Figure 4.7 You'll find HTML headings in the Style menu on the toolbar.

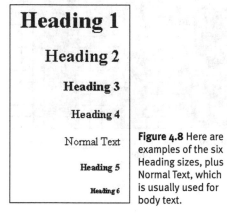

Figure 4.8 Here are examples of the six Heading sizes, plus Normal Text, which is usually used for body text.

Assigning HTML heading styles

HTML supplies six levels of *headings* that you can use to call attention to text on your Web pages. Think of headings as being similar to headlines in a newspaper. They're usually bigger than the body text on the page and are often bold. Headings are what's known as a *paragraph style*, so a line of white space may precede and follow a heading depending on how your Web administrator has set up your site. Heading styles are numbered, with Heading 1 being the largest and Heading 6 the smallest. Headings are selected from the Contribute Style menu on the Editing toolbar (**Figure 4.7**), or by choosing Format > Style. If your site administrator is using Cascading Style Sheets to format text on your site (see "Using CSS Styles," later in this chapter), these heading choices might not be available.

One other choice appears in the Style menu—Normal, for the style Normal Text, which is the text used for the body of your document (**Figure 4.8**).

To apply a heading style:

1. Click within the line you want to make into a heading to place the insertion point.

2. Select a heading size (1–6) from the Style menu in the Editing toolbar.

   or

   Choose Format > Style, then choose a heading style from the submenu.

   The text is formatted as a heading.

Coloring and highlighting text

You can select individual blocks of text and change their color, or you can apply a highlighting effect, in which the background of the text is colored.

To color text:

1. Select the text you want to color.

2. Click the Text Color button in the Editing toolbar (**Figure 4.9**).

   or

   Choose Format > Text Color.

   The color picker appears (**Figure 4.10**).

3. Click a color with the eyedropper to select it; it can be any color in the color picker or any color visible on your desktop or the page you are editing.

   When you select the color, the color picker closes and the text changes color.

To highlight text:

1. Select the text you want to highlight.

2. Click the Highlight Color button in the toolbar.

   or

   Choose Format > Highlight Color.

   The color picker appears.

3. Click a color with the eyedropper to select it; it can be any color in the color picker or any color visible on your desktop or the page you are editing.

   When you select the color, the color picker closes, and the text is highlighted the selected color.

✔ Tip

■ Pressing Esc closes the color picker without applying a color (Windows only).

Text Color

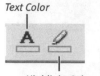

Figure 4.9 The Text Color and Highlight Color buttons on the Editing toolbar.

Highlight Color

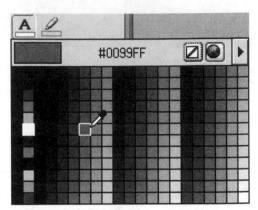

Figure 4.10 Use the eyedropper on the color picker to choose your new text color.

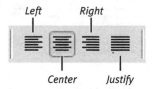

Left *Right*

Center *Justify*

Figure 4.11 The text-alignment buttons on the Editing toolbar.

Table 4.1

Alignment Shortcut Keys		
SHORTCUT KEY (WINDOWS)	SHORTCUT KEY (MAC)	WHAT IT DOES
Ctrl-Alt-Shift-L	Cmd-Opt-Shift-L	Left alignment
Ctrl-Alt-Shift-C	Cmd-Opt-Shift-C	Center alignment
Ctrl-Alt-Shift-R	Cmd-Opt-Shift-R	Right alignment
Ctrl-Alt-Shift-J	Cmd-Opt-Shift-J	Full justification

Setting text alignment

Contribute's similarity to a word processor continues with its ability to align text with the left margin, the right margin, or the center of the page. You can also justify text, which adds space as needed between words so that both the left and right margins are aligned.

To align text:

1. Select the text you want to align.

2. On the Editing toolbar, click the Left, Center, Right, or Justify button (**Figure 4.11**).

   or

   Choose Format > Align > and then choose Left, Center, Right, or Justify.

   You can also use the shortcut keys listed in **Table 4.1**.

   The text is aligned according to the option you clicked.

✔ Tip

- You can change the alignment for a single paragraph, a heading, or an entire page.

USING HTML STYLES

Indenting text

You can indent blocks of text in Contribute, but indenting works a little differently here than it does in a word processor. In Word, for example, an indent for a paragraph might pull the left margin of the paragraph in toward the center of the page and might further indent the first line of the paragraph, but would leave the right margin of the paragraph unchanged. The Indent command in Contribute indents the text of the paragraph from both margins (**Figure 4.12**).

To indent text:

1. Click within the paragraph you want to indent, or if you want to indent more than one paragraph, select the text.

2. Click the Indent button on the toolbar (**Figure 4.13**).

   or

   Choose Format > Indent, or press Ctrl-Alt-] (Cmd-Opt-]).

   You can increase indent levels by repeating this step.

To remove indents:

1. Click within the paragraph where you want to remove indenting, or if you want to affect more than one paragraph, select the text.

2. Click the Outdent button on the Editing toolbar.

   or

   Choose Format > Outdent, or press Ctrl-Alt-[(Cmd-Opt-[).

✔ Tips

■ You can often get better control over text placement by using tables rather than indenting. See Chapter 7, "Creating Tables," for more information.

launched by mid-2003, and the Government channel to follow at some future date that would be determined by mutual consultation.

Another possibility that I think that we should explore would be to launch our first channel with combined PEG programming, and plan to split the programming into two or more channels when needed. That would allow us to build interest among all segments of the community from the start, not just the educational crowd.

Figure 4.12 When you indent text, it is indented from both margins.

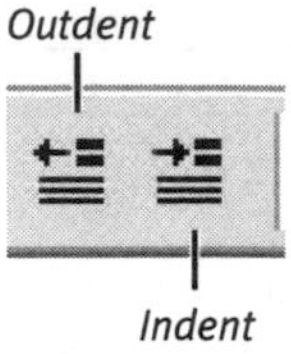

Figure 4.13 The Indent and Outdent buttons on the toolbar.

■ Contribute does its indenting by applying the HTML `<blockquote>` tag.

Using CSS Styles

From the standpoint of the site designer, the main benefit of using Cascading Style Sheet styles in a Web site is that with CSS, changing the definition of a style changes all the instances that have that style on the site. For example, imagine that a Web designer creates a CSS style named Caution Text that is used on dozens of pages on a site. The text is red, bold, and large (the equivalent of 24 points). After a bit of friendly counseling by his supervisor, the designer tones down Caution Text to be less visually obtrusive. Because the style is a CSS style, changing the definition of Caution Text in the style sheet automatically changes every use of Caution Text in the whole site.

Also, by using CSS styles, and by asking the site administrator to disable use of anything other than CSS styles, the designer can make sure that you, the Contribute user, don't have the ability to inadvertently mess up the site design by applying HTML headings, making text bold, or doing things the designer doesn't want. You'll only have the ability to add and edit text and images, which lets the designer sleep at night.

Contribute doesn't let you create CSS styles (you need Dreamweaver or a comparable tool to create style sheets), but you can use the CSS styles that are attached to the site templates. If the designer has created CSS styles, and you have the editing permission to also apply HTML styles, you should use the CSS styles in preference to the HTML styles. It makes your Web site easier to maintain, improves the site's performance for visitors, and makes it easier to change the site in the future, when the inevitable site redesign happens.

continues on next page

As you can see in **Figure 4.14**, the names of CSS styles appear in the Editing toolbar's Style menu along with the seven HTML styles (Normal plus Headings 1 through 6; in Figure 4.14, the site administrator had not disabled HTML styles). The figure also illustrates a drawback of the toolbar's Style menu—that the menu doesn't expand to display the entire name of the CSS style, should the name be longer than the menu is wide. The Style submenu of the Format menu shows the entire style name (**Figure 4.15**).

To apply CSS styles:

1. Click within the line you want to style to place the insertion point, or select the text you want to style.

2. Choose Format > Style, then select the CSS style from the Style submenu.

   or

   Choose a CSS style from the Style menu in the Editing toolbar.

Figure 4.14 When a site template includes CSS styles, they appear in the Editing toolbar's Style menu.

Figure 4.15 The Style submenu of the Format menu displays the full names of the CSS styles.

✔ Tips

- Besides giving finer control over the look of type, CSS styles are useful for positioning elements on the page. Don't be surprised if text moves around as you apply a CSS style to it.

- You can clear a style and return to the default text style for the page by selecting the text you want to change and then choosing Normal from the Style menu in the Editing toolbar.

- Some CSS styles are redefined HTML tags. For example, a designer can redefine the Heading 2 style to be a different font as well as bold, centered, and/or in a different text color. You still apply Heading 2 from the Editing toolbar's Style menu, but the effect is different.

- When you see links on Web pages that are not underlined, or are the same color as the body text but are bold, the trick was done using CSS styles.

- When you launch Contribute, it connects to each site for which you have a site connection and makes sure that those sites are using the latest versions of the templates on each of them. As part of the same process, Contribute reads the style sheets for the sites.

Working with Lists

Lists are an easy way to organize content on your Web page. Contribute supports three types of lists:

Numbered lists or Ordered lists, for lists with items that need to be in a particular order (**Figure 4.16**). List items are numbered and indented from the left margin. If you add or remove items from the numbered list, it automatically renumbers.

Bulleted lists or Unordered, for lists of items in no particular order (**Figure 4.17**).

Definition lists, where each item has an indented subitem (**Figure 4.18**).

To create a list:

1. Type the items for your list into the draft window. After typing each item, press Enter (Return).

2. Select the items in the list.

3. Choose Format > List, then choose Numbered List, Bulleted List, or Definition List from the submenu.

   or

   Click either the Numbered List or Bulleted List button in the Editing toolbar.

✔ Tip

■ At the end of your list, you can turn off the list function either by pressing Enter (Return) twice or by clicking the appropriate list button in the Editing toolbar.

Lucy Kaplansky Discography

1. The Tide (1994)
2. Flesh and Bone (1996)
3. Ten Year Night (1999)
4. Every Single Day (2001)

Lucy Kaplansky Discography

1. The Tide (1994)
2. Flesh and Bone (1996)
3. Cry Cry Cry (1998) w/ Richard Shindell, Dar Williams
4. Ten Year Night (1999)
5. Every Single Day (2001)

Figure 4.16 Numbered lists automatically renumber if you insert a new item between two existing items.

Global Survival Kit

- Metal box
- Survival knife
- Compass
- Fire starter
- Water bag
- Water purification tablets
- Rescue whistle
- Fishing and foraging kit

Figure 4.17 Bulleted lists are single-spaced and indented.

Excerpts from *The Devil's Dictionary*, by Ambrose Bierce
Originally published 1911 (copyright expired)

CHILDHOOD , n.
  The period of human life intermediate between the idiocy of infancy and the folly of youth -- two removes from the sin of manhood and three from the remorse of age.
DAWN , n.
  The time when men of reason go to bed. Certain old men prefer to rise at about that time, taking a cold bath and a long walk with an empty stomach, and otherwise mortifying the flesh.
DELIBERATION , n.
  The act of examining one's bread to determine which side it is buttered on.
NONSENSE , n.
  The objections that are urged against this excellent dictionary.
SCRIBBLER , n.
  A professional writer whose views are antagonistic to one's own.

Figure 4.18 Definition lists have the definitions indented under the definition terms. (The definition terms don't have to be all uppercase—they just happen to be in this figure.)

Figure 4.19 In the List Properties dialog, you can change the way lists are numbered and bulleted.

Table 4.2

List-Numbering Options	
List Name	**Example**
Number	1, 2, 3, 4 ...
Roman Small	i, ii, iii, iv ...
Roman Large	I, II, III, IV ...
Alphabet Small	a, b, c, d ...
Alphabet Large	A, B, C, D ...

Setting List Properties

Numbered lists and bulleted lists have properties you can change in Contribute. You can choose between five types of numbering, as shown in **Table 4.2**. For bulleted lists, you can choose either a round bullet (the default) or a square bullet. There are no properties to set for a definition list.

To set list properties:

1. Click in the list you want to change to place the insertion point.

2. Choose Format > List > Properties. The List Properties dialog appears (**Figure 4.19**).

3. Do one or more of the following:
   - ▲ In the "List type" pop-up menu, select Bulleted List, Numbered List, or Directory List ("definition list" is called "Directory List" in this dialog for some reason).
   - ▲ In the "Style" pop-up menu, select one of the Bulleted List or Numbered List styles.
   - ▲ Use the "Start at number" text box to set the value for the first item in the numbered list.

4. Click OK.

✔ Tip

- ■ You may notice that there is a fourth choice in the "List type" pop-up menu, called Menu List. That choice creates an unusual type of list that is based on the <menu> tag. That tag was deprecated—recommended that it not be used—when HTML 4.01 was standardized several years ago. I suggest that you avoid the use of the Menu List option.

Nesting lists

You can indent lists within lists to create *nested lists*. Because nested lists do not have to be of the same type, you can create, for example, a numbered list with an indented bulleted list, and you can have multiple levels of nested lists within one overall list (**Figure 4.20**).

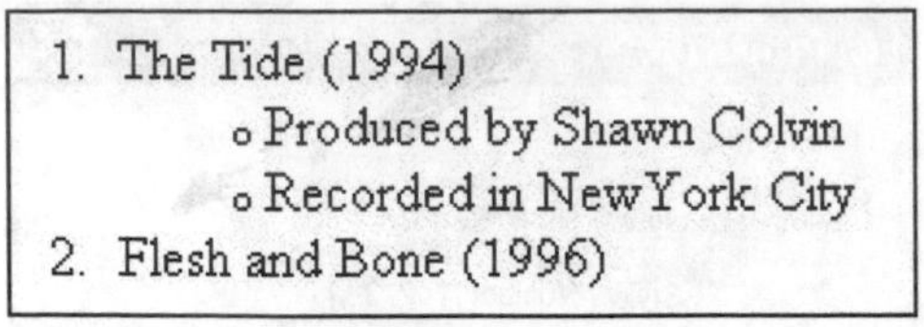

To create a nested list:

1. Click the end of a line within an existing list to place the insertion point.

2. Press Enter (Return).
   Contribute creates another line of the list.

3. Press Tab.
   Contribute creates a new indented sublist of the same type as the parent list. For example, if the parent list is a numbered list, the new sublist will also be a numbered list.

4. (Optional) If you want the sublist to be a different type of list than the parent list, click the Numbered List or Bulleted List button in the Editing toolbar.

5. Type the list item.

6. Press Enter (Return).
   Contribute creates a new sublist item.

7. Press the Enter (Return) key twice to leave the sublist.

✔ Tips

- You can also click the Outdent button in the Editing toolbar to merge the sublist back into the main list.

- You can use the List Properties dialog to format sublists as well as lists.

- If you are in a table and press Tab, Contribute will jump to the next cell, rather than indenting and creating a nested list. One workaround is to create the nested list outside of the table, cut it, then paste it in the table cell where you want it to go.

1. The Tide (1994)
   - Produced by Shawn Colvin
   - Recorded in New York City
2. Flesh and Bone (1996)

Figure 4.20 You can nest bulleted lists inside numbered lists.

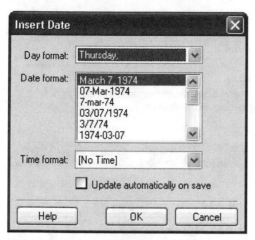

Figure 4.21 Contribute lets you insert dates into your draft pages in a variety of formats.

Inserting Dates

Contribute can insert the current date and time, in a variety of formats, into your Web page. You can choose whether or not to add the day of the week.

To insert the current date:

1. Click in your draft to place the insertion point where you want to date to appear.

2. Choose Insert > Date.

   The Insert Date dialog appears (**Figure 4.21**).

3. Do one or more of the following:
   ▲ If you want the day to appear, use the "Day format" pop-up menu to set the appearance of the day of the week.
   ▲ Make a selection from the "Date format" list.
   ▲ If you want the time to appear, choose the 12-hour or 24-hour format from the "Time format" list.
   ▲ Select the "Update automatically on save" check box, if you want that to happen. This is very useful if you want visitors to your site to know when the page was last updated.

4. Click OK.

   Contribute inserts the date (and possibly the time) into your draft page.

Adding Horizontal Rules

A *horizontal rule* is a line that runs across the page, providing a division between parts of the document (**Figure 4.22**). By default, a horizontal rule in Contribute is the width of the page, is 1 pixel high, and has a small drop shadow. You can change these properties if you want.

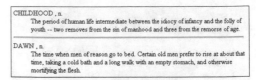

Figure 4.22 This horizontal rule separates two sections of the draft page.

To insert a horizontal rule:

1. Click in the page to place the insertion point where you want the horizontal rule to appear.

2. Choose Insert > Horizontal Rule.

A line appears as wide as the page.

To modify a horizontal rule's properties:

1. Click the horizontal rule to select it.

2. Right-click the horizontal rule, and then choose Properties from the shortcut menu.

The Horizontal Rule Properties dialog appears (**Figure 4.23**).

Figure 4.23 You can change the width and height of a horizontal rule in the Horizontal Rule Properties dialog.

3. Do one or more of the following:

▲ Type a number in the Width field, and choose either "pixels" or "percent" from the pop-up menu. Choosing "pixels" creates a fixed-width line; choosing "percent" creates a line that expands or contracts depending on the width of the site visitor's browser window.

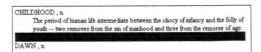

Figure 4.24 When you select the rule, you can see the white space above and below it.

▲ In the Height text box, type a number for the horizontal rule. This height is measured in pixels.

▲ If you select the Use Outline Shading check box, the line appears as an outline rather than as a solid line.

4. Click OK.

✔ Tips

■ The horizontal rule has white space above and below it, which you can see if you click the rule to select it (**Figure 4.24**).

■ Horizontal rules are a leftover from the early days of HTML. Use them sparingly, if at all, because they tend to make a page look dated.

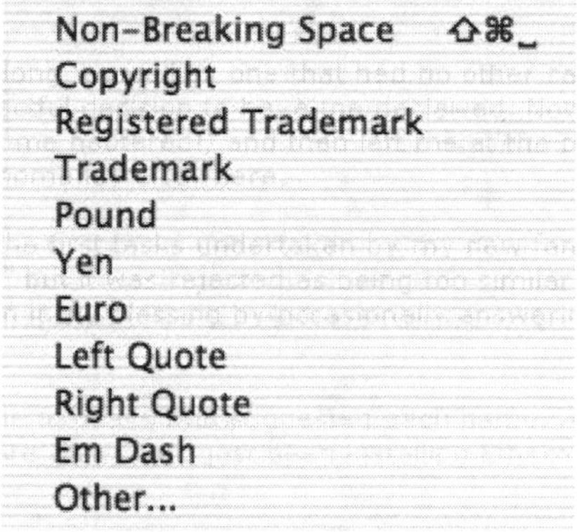

Non-Breaking Space ⇧⌘_
Copyright
Registered Trademark
Trademark
Pound
Yen
Euro
Left Quote
Right Quote
Em Dash
Other...

Figure 4.25 The most common special characters are available from the Insert > Special Characters submenu.

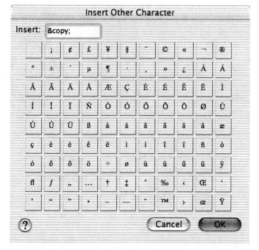

Figure 4.26 The Insert Other Character dialog provides the rest of the special characters Contribute can insert.

Inserting Special Characters

You can add special characters, such as the Euro, copyright, or trademark symbols, to your page in Contribute without having to remember their bizarre HTML equivalents. Relief is just a menu choice away.

To insert a special character:

1. Click in the page to place the insertion point where you want the special character to appear.

2. Choose Insert > Special Characters, then choose the special character you want from the submenu (**Figure 4.25**).

   or

   If the character you want doesn't appear in the menu, choose Other. The Insert Other Character dialog appears (**Figure 4.26**).

3. Click the character you want to use, then click OK to close the dialog.

   Contribute inserts the special character on your page.

✔ Tip

■ There's an interesting trick that you can do with the Insert Other Character dialog. When you click on a special character in the dialog, the character's HTML code appears in the field at the top of the dialog. You can also use this field to insert other HTML into your draft page, something that Contribute otherwise prevents you from doing. Just copy the HTML from a browser or text editor, open the Insert Other Character dialog, and paste into the text field. For example, you could paste in snippets of HTML from your other Web sites, or paste in small forms. You will need to use the keyboard equivalent for paste, as the menus are disabled while the dialog is open.

Finding and Replacing Text

Contribute has a fairly rudimentary Find and Replace feature that can search the current draft document for a particular piece of text and then replace that text with another.

To find text:

1. With the draft page you want to search displayed, choose Edit > Find, or press Ctrl-F (Cmd-F).

   The Find and Replace dialog appears (**Figure 4.27**).

2. In the "Search for" text box, type the text you're looking for.

3. (Optional) If you want to match the case pattern (uppercase or lowercase) of the text you type in the "Search for" text box, select the "Match case" check box.

4. Click Find Next.

   Contribute searches the draft, and if the text is found, it highlights the text in the document window. If Contribute does not find the text, a dialog appears telling you so.

5. If you want to continue searching, click Find Next again. Otherwise, click Close.

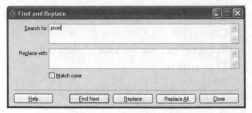

Figure 4.27 Contribute can find and replace text on your draft page.

To find and replace text:

1. With the draft page you want to search displayed, choose Edit > Find, or press Ctrl-F (Cmd-F).

   The Find and Replace dialog appears.

2. In the "Search for" field, type the text you're looking for.

3. (Optional) If you want to match the case pattern (uppercase or lowercase) of the text you type in the "Search for" text box, select the "Match case" check box.

4. Type the text you want as the replacement in the "Replace with" text box.

5. Click Find Next. Contribute finds the first instance of the search text.

6. Click Replace.

7. (Optional) If you want to have Contribute automatically replace all the found text with the contents of the "Replace with" text box, click Replace All.

   Contribute displays a dialog telling you how many replacements were made.

8. Click Close to return to the draft window.

FINDING AND REPLACING TEXT

Checking Spelling

No word processor comes without a spelling checker these days, and neither does Contribute. You can check the spelling on a draft page and add words to Contribute's spelling checker in a personal dictionary.

To spell-check your draft:

1. With the draft page you want to spell-check displayed, click the Check Spelling button on the Editing toolbar (**Figure 4.28**), or choose Format > Check Spelling or press F7 (Windows only).

   If Contribute finds a word it believes is spelled incorrectly, the Check Spelling dialog appears (**Figure 4.29**).

2. Click Add to Personal if the word Contribute found is correct and you want to add it to your personal dictionary so that Contribute doesn't flag it as an error again.

   or

   Click Ignore to tell the spelling checker to ignore this instance of the word, or Ignore All to ignore the word throughout the document.

   or

   Select a replacement from the "Suggestions" list, or type the replacement in the "Change to" text box. Then click the Change button, or click Change All to replace the word throughout the document.

3. When the spelling check is finished, click Close.

✔ Tip

■ Even if you place the insertion point in the draft page, the spelling checker always starts at the top of the page.

Figure 4.28 Trigger the spelling checker with the Check Spelling button on the Editing toolbar.

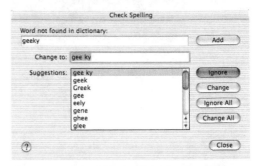

Figure 4.29 Click Add in the Check Spelling dialog to add an unknown word (such as your last name) to Contribute's personal dictionary.

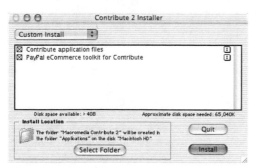

Figure 4.30 If you didn't install the PayPal e-commerce toolkit when you first installed Contribute 2, you'll need to reinstall contribute and also select the PayPal toolkit option.

Adding PayPal E-commerce Buttons

One of the new features in Contribute 2 is the capability to add buttons to your Web pages that allow the user to purchase products and services from your Web site. These buttons work with PayPal, one of the largest online payment services. PayPal allows anyone with an email address to securely send and receive payments online; to send money, the source of the funds can be a credit card, a bank account, or a balance in the purchaser's PayPal account. By clicking a PayPal button on your site, the visitor is directed to a secure form on the PayPal site that takes their payment information and allows them to complete the purchase. Then PayPal deposits the money from the purchase into your PayPal account, from which you can later transfer the funds to your regular checking account.

When you first installed Contribute 2, you had the option to install the PayPal e-commerce toolkit. If you didn't install the toolkit at that time, you can do it now, but you'll need to reinstall Contribute, and select the option to install the PayPal e-commerce toolkit (**Figure 4.30**). If you need more help with installation, see Chapter 1, "Getting Started."

✔ Tips

- In order to accept credit card payments via PayPal, you must have a Business or Premier PayPal account. PayPal charges you a fee for receiving credit card payments. At press time, these fees ranged from 2.2% to 2.9% of the transaction amount, plus $.30 per transaction.

- The PayPal e-commerce toolkit is actually an extension to Contribute written by WebAssist (http://www.webassist.com), based on their similar toolkit for Macromedia Dreamweaver MX. You can find out technical details about both the Contribute and Dreamweaver toolkits at the WebAssist Web site.

- If you reinstall Contribute, you will lose any draft pages that you were working on, though your site connections and preferences are preserved. You should publish or cancel any drafts before you reinstall the program.

- Before you can accept payments via PayPal, you will need to sign up for a PayPal account, if you don't already have one. You can do that at http://www.paypal.com.

Types of E-commerce transactions

The PayPal e-commerce toolkit allows you to place four different kinds of buttons on your Web pages for electronic transactions:

◆ A **Buy Now Button** allows you to sell individual items from your Web site. The user clicks the button, and is taken to a payment form on the PayPal Web site. When the user completes the payment, he or she can optionally be sent back to your site to continue browsing.

◆ An **Add to Cart Button** is useful if you have multiple items that you are selling from your site. When the user clicks this button, they are taken to a shopping cart page on the PayPal site. At that point they can choose to go through the checkout process, or return to your site and add more items to the shopping cart.

◆ The **View Cart Button** works with the Add to Cart Button to allow your site visitors to view the contents of their shopping cart.

◆ A **Subscription Button** allows you to sell ongoing subscriptions from your Web site. From the e-commerce standpoint, a subscription consists of two or more payments made at a regular interval, such as days, weeks, months, or years. For example, you could use a Subscription Button to allow your site visitors to pay for a monthly newsletter you send out via email, to renew annual dues for a club, or to make recurring donations to a community group.

Choosing any of these transaction types from the PayPal pop-up menu in the Editing toolbar displays a Wizard that steps you through setting up the transaction.

Figure 4.31 On the first page of any of the PayPal Wizards, you must enter your PayPal account name, which is the email address that you have registered with PayPal.

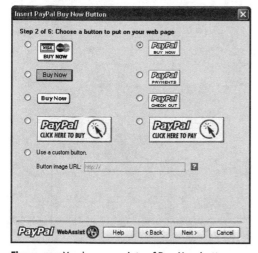

Figure 4.32 You have a variety of Buy Now buttons from which to choose.

To add a Buy Now button:

1. On a draft page, click to place the insertion point where you want the button.

2. From the PayPal pop-up menu in the toolbar, choose Buy Now Button.

   The first screen of the Insert PayPal Buy Now Button Wizard appears (**Figure 4.31**).

3. Type in the name of your PayPal account, which is the email address that you used to register with PayPal, then click Next.

   The Choose a Button screen appears (**Figure 4.32**).

4. Click a button next to the button image that you wish to use for your Buy Now button.

   Alternatively, you can click "Use a custom button," then enter the URL to a button image on your site.

continues on next page

5. Click Next.

The Item Details screen appears (**Figure 4.33**).

6. Do the following (all entries on this screen are optional, but recommended):

▲ In the "Item name/service" field, enter the name of the item or service that you are selling.

▲ In the "Item ID/number" field, enter an item number or product code.

▲ In the "Price of item/service" field, enter an amount. You must include a decimal amount, i.e., you must type a number like 15.00, not just 15. Don't type a currency symbol.

You may also leave this field blank, which will allow the purchaser to enter their own price when they get to the PayPal payment form. This is useful for payments such as donations.

▲ Choose the currency for the payment amount from the pop-up menu. Your choices are US Dollars, Canadian Dollars, Euros, Pounds Sterling, or Yen.

▲ If you are willing to allow the purchaser to buy more than one of the items or services, select the check box.

7. Click Next.

The Shipping Preferences screen appears (**Figure 4.34**).

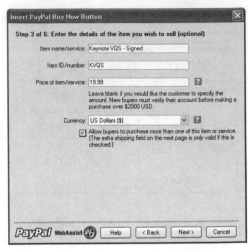

Figure 4.33 The Item Details screen allows you to enter the name of the item or service and its price.

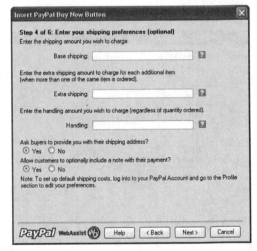

Figure 4.34 If you charge for shipping, enter the shipping amounts here.

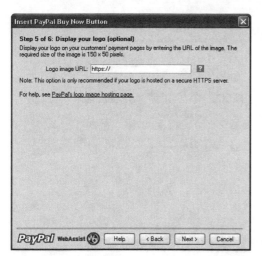

Figure 4.35 If you want to put your company brand on the PayPal payments screen, enter the URL of the logo image on this screen.

8. Do the following (again, the entries on this screen are optional):

   ▲ If the item you are selling has a shipping charge, type it in the "Base shipping" field.

   ▲ If the purchaser orders more than one item, you probably need to impose additional shipping charges for each item. Enter that charge in the "Extra shipping" field.

   ▲ If you'll be adding a handling fee, type the amount in the "Handling" field. Handling fees are calculated once per order as a flat fee.

   ▲ If you want the buyer to provide you with their shipping address, select the Yes button next to "Ask buyers to provide you with their shipping address?" If you don't need the buyer's address (perhaps because they are purchasing an item that they can download, or because they are purchasing a service), click No.

   ▲ Select Yes or No to the question "Allow customers to optionally include a note with their payment?"

9. Click Next.

   The Display Your Logo screen appears (**Figure 4.35**).

   continues on next page

ADDING PAYPAL E-COMMERCE BUTTONS

10. If you want your logo to appear on the PayPal payments page, type the URL for the logo image. Your logo should be hosted on a secure server (see the sidebar "Staying Secure"). This is another optional entry.

The logo image must be exactly 150 by 50 pixels in size.

11. Click Next.

The Customize Customer Experience screen appears (**Figure 4.36**). This screen allows you to send your customers to two different places depending on whether their transaction is successful or canceled.

12. Do the following (the entries on this screen are optional, but recommended):

▲ Type the Success URL. This is a page that your customers will be sent to if the transaction is successfully completed. For example, you might want to send your customers to a page thanking them for the purchase.

▲ Type the Cancel Payment URL. This is a page that your customers will be sent to if the transaction fails for any reason. Possible reasons could include failure to validate a credit card, or if the buyer cancels the transaction before completing the purchase process.

13. Click Next.

The Summary screen appears (**Figure 4.37**). Review the information, and if needed, click the Back button to make any changes.

14. Click Finish.

The Buy Now button appears on your draft page (**Figure 4.38**).

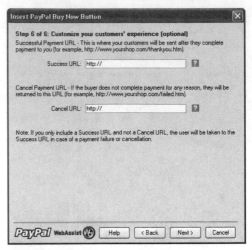

Figure 4.36 It is a good idea to enter URLs on this screen that direct your customer to pages letting them know that their transaction has succeeded, or that it has not.

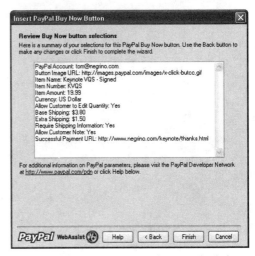

Figure 4.37 The Summary screen lets you check that all the details are correct before creating your Buy Now button.

Figure 4.38 The finished Buy Now button uses the button image that you selected from the Wizard.

Staying Secure

Putting your logo on the PayPal payments page is a good way to look more professional, but to do it right, you will need to host the logo image on a secure Web server. That's a server that encrypts all of the data it sends for security purposes. Technically, you don't have to host your logo image securely, but most browsers will present a security alert to the buyer (**Figure 4.39**). Worse, that alert will appear every time they add an item to the shopping cart, and when they check out. Buyers are rightly suspicious when they are sending money online and the browser alerts them that the transaction may not be fully secure.

There are a variety of services that will host your logo file on a secure server inexpensively, often for $1 per image per month or less. Some of these services are:

◆ PushPic.com (`http://www.pushpic.com/`)

◆ SSLPal (`http://www.sslpal.com/`)

◆ ImageWiz.net (`http://www.imagewiz.net/`)

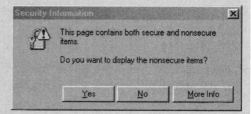

Figure 4.39 This security alert will annoy your potential customers—and probably drive away sales—if you don't host your logo on a secure Web server.

To add an Add to Cart button:

1. On a draft page, click to place the insertion point where you want the button.

2. From the PayPal pop-up menu in the toolbar, choose Add to Cart Button.

   The first screen of the Insert PayPal Add to Cart Button Wizard appears (**Figure 4.40**).

3. Type in the name of your PayPal account, which is the email address that you used to register with PayPal.

4. Click Next.

   The Choose a Button screen appears (**Figure 4.41**).

5. Click a button next to the button image that you wish to use for your Add to Cart button.

   Alternatively, you can click "Use a custom button," then enter the URL to a button image on your site.

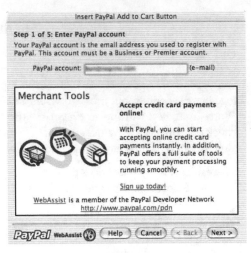

Figure 4.40 Begin adding an Add to Cart button to your page by entering your PayPal account name.

Figure 4.41 Choose the Add to Cart button that you want.

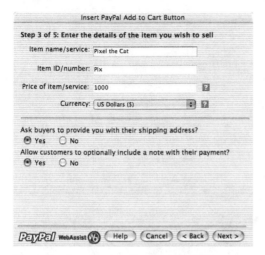

Figure 4.42 Enter the item details that will later appear in the shopping cart.

6. Click Next.

The Item Details screen appears (**Figure 4.42**).

7. Do the following (all entries on this screen are optional, but recommended):

▲ In the "Item name/service" field, enter the name of the item or service that you are selling.

▲ In the "Item ID/number" field, enter an item number or product code.

▲ In the "Price of item/service" field, enter an amount. You must include a decimal amount, i.e., you must type a number like 15.00, not just 15. Don't type a currency symbol.

▲ Choose the currency for the payment amount from the pop-up menu. Your choices are US Dollars, Canadian Dollars, Euros, Pounds Sterling, or Yen.

▲ If you want the buyer to provide you with their shipping address, select the Yes button next to "Ask buyers to provide you with their shipping address?" If you don't need the buyer's address (perhaps because they are purchasing an item that they can download, or because they are purchasing a service), click No.

▲ Select Yes or No to the question "Allow customers to optionally include a note with their payment?"

7. Click Next.

The Display Your Logo screen appears.

8. (Optional) If you want your logo to appear on the PayPal payments page, type its URL. Your logo should be hosted on a secure server.

9. Click Next.

The Customize Customer Experience screen appears.

continues on next page

10. Do the following (entries on this screen are optional, but recommended):

▲ Type the Success URL. This is a page that your customers will be sent to if the transaction is successfully completed. For example, you might want to send your customers to a page thanking them for the purchase.

▲ Type the Cancel Payment URL. This is a page that your customers will be sent to if the transaction fails for any reason. Possible reasons could include failure to validate a credit card, or if the buyer cancels the transaction before completing the purchase process.

11. Click Next.

The Summary screen appears (**Figure 4.43**). Review the information, and if needed, click the Back button to make any changes.

12. Click Finish.

The Add to Cart button appears on your draft page (**Figure 4.44**).

Figure 4.43 Check the Summary screen carefully, because you can't edit a PayPal button once you create it; you can only delete it and start over.

Figure 4.44 The completed Add to Cart button.

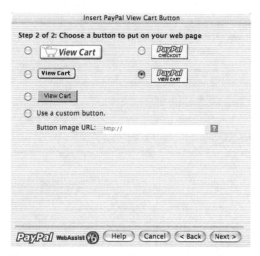

Figure 4.45 You have only five preset choices for a View Cart button.

 Figure 4.46 This View Cart button is stylistically similar to the Add to Cart button.

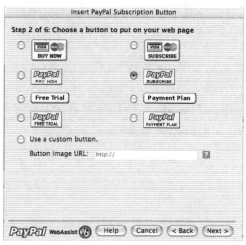

Figure 4.47 Choose the Subscription button that you want.

To add a View Cart button:

1. On a draft page, click to place the insertion point where you want the button.

2. From the PayPal pop-up menu in the toolbar, choose View Cart Button.

   The first screen of the Insert PayPal View Cart Button Wizard appears.

3. Type in the name of your PayPal account, which is the email address that you used to register with PayPal.

4. Click Next.

   The Choose a Button screen appears (**Figure 4.45**).

5. Click a button next to the button image that you wish to use for your View Cart button.

   Alternatively, you can click "Use a custom button," then enter the URL to a button image on your site.

6. Click Next.

   The Summary screen appears.

7. Click Finish.

   The View Cart button appears on your draft page (**Figure 4.46**).

To add a Subscription button:

1. On a draft page, click to place the insertion point where you want the button.

2. From the PayPal pop-up menu in the toolbar, choose Subscription Button.

   The first screen of the Insert PayPal Subscription Button Wizard appears.

3. Type in the name of your PayPal account, which is the email address that you used to register with PayPal.

4. Click Next.

   The Choose a Button screen appears (**Figure 4.47**).

continues on next page

5. Click a button next to the button image that you wish to use for your Subscription button.

Alternatively, you can click "Use a custom button," then enter the URL to a button image on your site.

6. Click Next.

The Subscription Details screen appears (**Figure 4.48**).

7. Do the following:

▲ (Optional) Type a subscription name. This is that name for the subscription that will appear on the PayPal payments page.

▲ (Optional) Type a Reference ID, if you use them.

▲ Choose the currency for the payment amount from the pop-up menu. Your choices are US Dollars, Canadian Dollars, Euros, Pounds Sterling, or Yen.

▲ In the Billing/Payment Plan section, type a number in the field next to "Charge customers." This will be the recurring amount.

▲ Choose the time period for the recurring payment from the two pop-up menus. Your choices are 1 to 30 and days, weeks, months, or years.

▲ Select either "Charge customers until they cancel" or "Stop charging after X payments," where X is the choice you make from the pop-up menu.

▲ If you want to offer your subscribers a free trial offer, or charge a setup fee, type a number and choose from the pop-up menus.

8. Click Next.

The Additional Subscription Details screen appears (**Figure 4.49**).

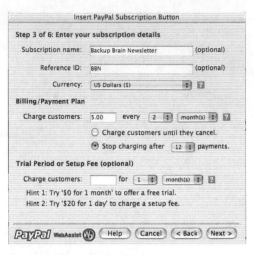

Figure 4.48 Enter the details of the subscription, and decide whether you want to offer a free trial period for your subscription.

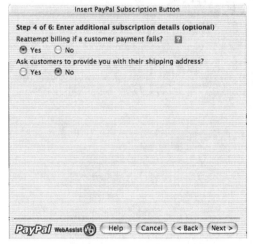

Figure 4.49 PayPal needs to know what to do if a customer payment fails.

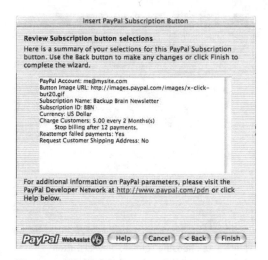

Figure 4.50 The Summary screen helps you prevent mistakes when setting up your subscription.

Figure 4.51 The completed Subscription button.

9. Answer the questions "Reattempt billing if a customer payment fails?" and "Ask customers to provide you with their shipping address?" by selecting the Yes or No buttons.

10. Click Next.

    The Display Your Logo screen appears.

11. (Optional) If you want your logo to appear on the PayPal payments page, type its URL. Your logo should be hosted on a secure server.

12. Click Next.

    The Customize Customer Experience screen appears.

13. Do the following (entries here are optional, but recommended):

    ▲ Type the Success URL. This is a page that your customers will be sent to if the transaction is successfully completed. For example, you might want to send your customers to a page thanking them for the purchase.

    ▲ Type the Cancel Payment URL. This is a page that your customers will be sent to if the transaction fails for any reason. Possible reasons could include failure to validate a credit card, or if the buyer cancels the transaction before completing the purchase process.

14. Click Next.

    The Summary screen appears (**Figure 4.50**). Review the information, and if needed, click the Back button to make any changes.

15. Click Finish.

    The Subscription button appears on your draft page (**Figure 4.51**).

To change the properties of a PayPal button:

1. On the draft page, click the button to select it.

2. Choose Format > PayPal Button Properties.

   A dialog opens that allows you to change the button's properties (**Figure 4.52**).

3. Make the needed changes, then click OK.

To remove a PayPal button:

1. On the draft page, click the button to select it.

2. Press Backspace (Delete).

   The button disappears from the page.

✔ Tip

■ If you are going to edit pages with PayPal buttons, you must ensure the PayPal extension is installed.

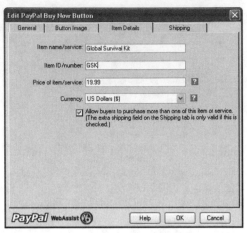

Figure 4.52 Choosing Format > PayPal Button Properties will bring up one of four dialogs, depending on the type of PayPal button you are modifying. This example is for the Buy Now button.

WORKING
WITH IMAGES

Images and media files convey an important amount of the information on your Web site. Although you'll probably get most of your message across with text (I guess it's not surprising that a writer would say that), graphics can provide a great deal of visual interest, and attractive graphics go a long way toward bringing visitors back to your site.

On the other hand, we've all seen Web sites that suffer from graphic overkill. It's always a bad sign when visitors to your site clutch their faces and scream, "My eyes! My eyes! *Aieeee!*" So while Macromedia Contribute makes it easy to add images and media files to your Web pages, don't forget that less is often more when it comes to Web design.

Adding Images to Your Pages

If you can access an image either locally or on one of your Web sites, Contribute can place it in your draft Web pages. You can insert images from your hard drive, your local network, or other applications; reuse an image from elsewhere on your Web site; or use an image from another Contribute draft page. However, Contribute has slightly different techniques for inserting images from your computer or inserting images from your Web site.

To insert images from your computer:

1. Begin editing the page where you want to place the image. For more information on how to begin editing pages, see Chapter 3, "Building Web Pages.".

   If the page you're editing is based on a template, the template will most likely have a place for the image to go and perhaps even a placeholder image (**Figure 5.1**). If the page contains a placeholder image that you want to replace with the new image, you should first delete the placeholder image by clicking it and pressing Backspace (Delete), or by choosing Edit > Clear.

2. Place the insertion point where you want the image to appear, and then choose Insert > Image > From My Computer, or press Ctrl-Alt-I (Cmd-Opt-I). You can also use the Image button on the toolbar, which when clicked will display a pop-up menu. Pick "From My Computer" from the pop-up menu.

   The Select Image dialog appears (**Figure 5.2**).

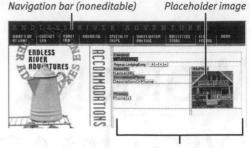

Navigation bar (noneditable)   Placeholder image

Editable template area

Figure 5.1 This is a new page, based on a Dreamweaver template, that is being edited in Contribute. Note that only part of the page can be edited and that the image on the page is there only as a placeholder.

Figure 5.2 In the Select Image dialog, choose the image you want to place on the page. The Windows version (top) allows you to view more photos at a time than the Mac version (bottom).

ADDING IMAGES TO YOUR PAGES

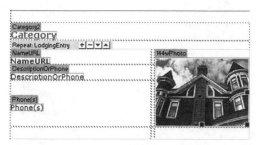

Figure 5.3 The new image goes where the placeholder image was.

Figure 5.4 The Choose Image on Website dialog allows you to browse the files on your Web sites, rather than on your computer.

Figure 5.5 The Preview section of the dialog makes it easier to find the image you want.

3. Navigate to the image file you want to insert, select it in the Select Image dialog, and click the Select button.

The image appears on your draft Web page (**Figure 5.3**).

To insert images from your Web site:

1. Begin editing the page where you want to place the image.

2. Place the insertion point where you want the image to appear, and then choose Insert > Image > From Website. You can also use the Image button on the toolbar, which when clicked will display a pop-up menu. Pick "From Website" from the pop-up menu.

The Choose Image on Website dialog appears (**Figure 5.4**). Rather than browsing through the folder structure on your hard drive, this dialog browses the folder structure from the Web sites you have defined as Connections in Contribute. Each defined site appears in the dialog.

3. Double-click the Web site that contains the image you want, then find and select the image file.

Contribute shows you a preview of the image you are browsing (**Figure 5.5**).

4. Click OK to insert the image into your Web page.

✔ Tips

- You can also add images to your Web pages by dragging and dropping them from most applications directly into the draft Web page in Contribute. Not all applications let you do this (unfortunately, you can't drag and drop from Macromedia's own Fireworks), but you can drag images from any of the Microsoft Office applications, Internet Explorer, or directly from the Mac or Windows desktop. If you're not sure whether drag and drop works from a particular program into Contribute, just try it. You may need to resize the windows of either Contribute or the other application in order to see both images onscreen at the same time.

- Another handy way to add a graphic to pages in Contribute is to copy the image from another application (such as such as a Web browser), and then paste it into your draft Web page.

- Normally, when you place an image file on a draft Web page that resides on your local hard drive or your network, Contribute uploads a copy of the image to the server when you publish the page. But what if the image is already on your server (because you used the image on another page)? Contribute recognizes that the file is already part of your Web site and doesn't upload another copy of the image file.

- The site administrator can specify that Contribute always prompt you to enter *alternative* descriptive text (sometimes known as the ALT tag) whenever you insert an image. This alternative text is used when the Web browser viewing the page has disabled viewing images, or used with alternative Web browsers designed for people with visual disabilities.

Image Types

To be used in Contribute, an image must already be in one of the three Web-ready graphic formats:

- ◆ JPEG
- ◆ GIF
- ◆ PNG

If the image is in another graphic format, such as BMP (a Windows format) or TIF, you must convert it to one of the Web-ready formats before attempting to place it in Contribute. To do the conversion, you need an image-editing program, such as Macromedia Fireworks or Adobe Photoshop. If you're looking for lower-cost programs, try Microsoft Paint on Windows computers and Graphic Converter on Macs.

To delete images:

1. In your draft Web page, select the image you want to delete.

2. Press Bksp (Delete), or choose Edit > Clear.

✔ Tip

- If you accidentally delete an image, you can get it back by choosing Edit > Undo Image or by pressing Ctrl-Z (Cmd-Z). Contribute can, by default, undo the last 50 actions.

Where Do the Images Go?

When you add images to Contribute pages, Contribute automatically creates a subdirectory of the current directory on your Web server (the one that contains the page that references the new image) called images, and uploads the images for that page to the images directory. Contribute also places images for any other pages in the current directory in the images subdirectory.

If you already have an images directory inside the current directory on the server, Contribute copies the new image to that images directory. Contribute does all this file-handling automatically for you. Unfortunately, Contribute doesn't allow you to specify where new images are to be placed on the server, so you can't have a single, separate images directory on the same level as your pages directory.

Adjusting Image Properties

After you have added an image to a page, you can modify the image properties. You can change the image; change the image size; change the image alignment and border; and change the image descriptive, or alternative, text (ALT text).

To modify image properties:

1. While editing a draft page, double-click the image you want to modify.

   or

   with the image selected, choose Format > Image Properties.

   or

   Right-click the image, and then choose Image Properties from the shortcut menu.

   Regardless of the method used, the Image Properties dialog appears (**Figure 5.6**).

2. Make the changes you want. See **Table 5.1** for details about each of the controls in the Image Properties dialog.

3. Click OK.

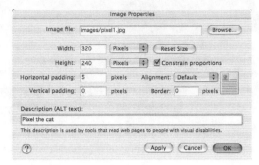

Figure 5.6 You can change many image attributes in the Image Properties dialog.

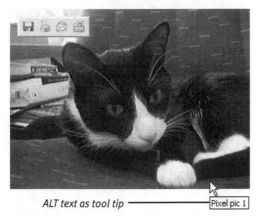

ALT text as tool tip ————————— Pixel pic 1

Figure 5.7 ALT text appears as a pop-up tool tip in many Web browsers.

✔ Tips

- You can add a border around an image with the Image Properties dialog, but Contribute offers no way to change the border color from the default color of black.

- It's a good idea to add ALT text to all of your images. Not only will ALT text make your pages more accessible for the disabled, but it might also be easier for your pages to be read by people who are using small-screen devices, such as mobile phones. Many browsers also show the ALT text displayed as a tool tip when the user mouses over the image (**Figure 5.7**).

Table 5.1

Image Properties Dialog	
PROPERTY OR CONTROL	WHAT IT DOES
Image file	Shows the path to the image file. The Browse button next to this field is a pop-up menu that allows you to find and select image files on your Web sites or files on your computer.
Width	Sets the width of the image file. You can choose the width either in pixels or as a percentage of the current image size from the pop-up menu next to this field.
Height	Sets the height of the image file. You can choose the height either in pixels or as a percentage of the current image size from the pop-up menu next to this field.
Reset Size	Returns the image to its original size if you have made changes.
Constrain proportions	Makes sure that changes to width or height are proportional. For example, if you increase the image width by 50%, its height will also increase by 50%.
Horizontal padding	Sets the amount of horizontal blank space to the left and right of the image, in pixels.
Vertical padding	Sets the amount of vertical blank space at the top and bottom of the image, in pixels.
Alignment	Sets the location of the image on the page in relation to text around the image. The pop-up menu choices are Default, which aligns the bottom of the image with the baseline of the text or the nearest object; Left; Right; Middle, which aligns the middle of the image with the text baseline; or Top, which aligns the image top with the top of the nearest object on the page. The graphic to the right of the pop-up menu changes to show you the effects of each choice.
Border	Sets the width of the border around the image, in pixels.
Description (ALT text)	Allows you to provide text that describes the image for browsers with images turned off, or for people with visual disabilities who use text-to-speech browsers.

ADJUSTING IMAGE PROPERTIES

Resizing images

You resize images in Contribute by dragging image selection handles, or if you want more precise control, by specifying a height or width in the Image Properties dialog.

To resize an image:

1. Select the image.

2. Click one of the image selection handles, and drag the handle until the image is the desired size (**Figure 5.8**).

   Holding down Shift while you drag the handle constrains the proportions of the image so that it isn't distorted as you resize it.

   or

   Double-click the image, and then change its height or width in the Image Properties dialog that appears (**Figure 5.6**). You can specify height and width values either as dimensions measured in pixels or as a percentage of the image size.

   Select the "Constrain proportions" check box to prevent the image from being distorted.

✔ Tip

■ Contribute's ability to resize images smoothly is limited. You will often get better results using an actual image-editing application, such as Macromedia Fireworks or Adobe Photoshop, to resize images *before* you use them in Contribute.

Figure 5.8 When you drag image selection handles to resize the image, the dotted line shows you what the new size of the image will be when you release the mouse button.

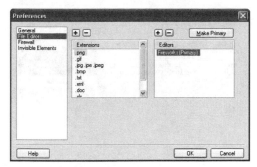

Figure 5.9 Use Contribute's File Editors preferences to select an external editor for a given image type.

Editing Images

Contribute doesn't allow you to edit images directly, other than resizing them. Instead, it hands off the editing task to another program on your computer, such as the default Fireworks. If you want to specify another program for image editing, such as Adobe Photoshop, you can do so in the File Editors category of Contribute's Preferences (**Figure 5.9**). Choose Edit > Preferences (Contribute > Preferences), select the File Editors category, and then make your selection.

When you tell Contribute to edit an image file already on one of your Web pages, Contribute uses the external editing program to edit the copy of the file on your Web server. If the file also exists as the original source file on your hard drive, it will not be edited, and changes to the original source file will not be automatically reflected in Contribute. Here's an example. If you build a Web page that contains the image file kitten.jpg, when you publish the page, Contribute makes a copy of the kitten.jpg file and uploads that copy to the server. If you then go back and edit the page using Contribute and edit the kitten.jpg file, the file you're editing is the copy of kitten.jpg on the server.

✔ Tip

■ When setting File Editors preferences, you can add image types to the list by clicking the plus button above the Extensions list. For each image type, you can also choose multiple external editors by clicking the plus button above the Editors column. When you select an editor from the list and click the Make Primary button, Contribute makes that external editor the preferred editor for the selected image type.

EDITING IMAGES

111

To edit an image

1. In Contribute's Edit mode, right-click
(Ctrl-click) the image you want to edit,
and choose Edit Image from the shortcut
menu (**Figure 5.10**).

Contribute creates a new draft page that
contains only the image, then displays a
window titled Editing Draft in Another
Application (**Figure 5.11**), and launches
the external editing program specified in
Contribute's Preferences.

If you're using Macromedia Fireworks as
the editing application, Fireworks displays the Find Source dialog, asking if you
want to edit a source file for the image,
that is, a copy of the file that's elsewhere
on your hard disk (**Figure 5.12**). In this
case, you want to edit the file on the
server, so click No.

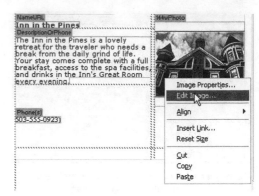

Figure 5.10 Begin editing an image by right-clicking it
(on Mac, Ctrl-click) and choosing Edit Image from the
shortcut menu.

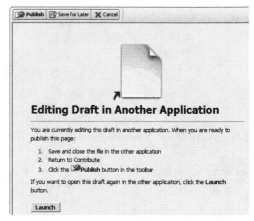

Figure 5.11 After you click the Edit button, Contribute
launches the external image editor and displays this
informational window.

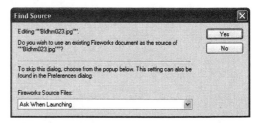

Figure 5.12 If you're using Fireworks as your image
editor, it asks if you want to edit the source file rather
than Contribute's copy on the server.

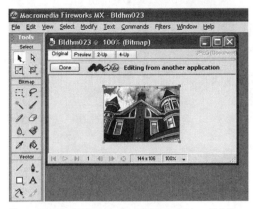

Figure 5.13 In the Fireworks editing window, click the Done button to save the file and return to Contribute.

Figure 5.14 Use the Contribute Pages panel to return to the draft page you are editing.

2. Make your changes to the image in the external editing application. If you're using Fireworks, click the Done button in the editing window when you're finished (**Figure 5.13**). If you're using another program, save and close the file when you are finished editing.

3. Switch back to Contribute.

Contribute still displays the page titled Editing Draft in Another Application.

4. Click Publish in the toolbar to save the edited image to the Web site.

Contribute returns to Browse mode and displays the page that contains only the now-changed image.

5. To continue editing the draft of the original page that contains the changed image, click its name in Contribute's Pages panel (**Figure 5.14**).

Replacing images

In the preceding scenario, you're making changes to a copy of the original source file on your Web site. But what if you make changes to the actual source file, and then want to replace the copy of the file on the Web server with a new copy of the changed source file? You cannot simply edit the page that the image file is on and replace the image, because Contribute will not overwrite files with the same name. As a safety measure, Contribute has a feature called *filename collision* that automatically renames a file if that file has the same name as a file already on the server. In this case, however, Contribute is being a little too clever; you want to overwrite files, because you probably don't want several versions of a file sitting on your Web server. Instead, you have to manually delete the old version of the file and replace it with the new version.

Understanding Contribute's Filename Collision

Because Macromedia designed Contribute to be extremely easy to use, even for people who have never edited Web pages before, it attempts to shield you from many of the details of working with files on your Web site. One of the things the program does is to automatically rename files that have identical filenames already on the server. This renaming process avoids filename collision without asking the user to choose another filename when you publish the draft page. Contribute does this by adding numbers to the end of the filename. For example, if you already have a file named `incrediblepicture.jpg` on your site, and you attempt to add another image with the same name, Contribute automatically (and without letting you know) renames the new version `incrediblepicture_000.jpg` when you click the Publish button.

As you repeatedly edit pages, you can end up with several differently named copies of nearly identical files, only one of which you are actually using on a page. Using Dreamweaver, the site administrator can delete unwanted duplicate files.

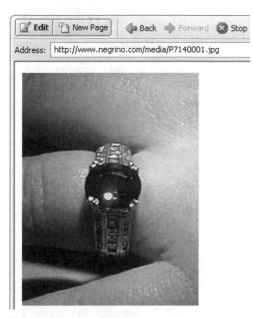

Address: http://www.negrino.com/media/P7140001.jpg

Figure 5.15 Browse to the image you want to replace so that it appears alone.

✔ Tip

- If the image you are replacing appears on other pages on your site, it is very important that the image have exactly the same name and be located in exactly the same place on the Web server as the image you are replacing. This can be tricky to accomplish with Contribute. Usually, you should use a more powerful product like Dreamweaver to make any changes that affect multiple pages on your Web site. Be especially careful of deleting files from the site unless you are certain it is safe to do so.

To replace an image with another image of the same name:

1. Use Contribute's browser to browse directly to the image file so that it appears by itself in the Contribute window (**Figure 5.15**).

   To do this, you need the entire URL of the image, such as `http://www.mysite.com/images/picture.jpg`.

2. Choose File > Delete Page.

   If Delete Page is disabled, your site administrator has not enabled you to delete editable files. Contact your site administrator, or if you are the site administrator, see "Assigning permissions" in Chapter 10 for more information.

3. Browse to a page that used the now-deleted image.

   The page displays a broken image icon where the image was.

4. Click Edit Page on the toolbar.

5. Choose Insert > Image > From My Computer (or Insert > Image > From Website).

   The appropriate image selection dialog appears.

6. Navigate to the new version of the image, select it in the dialog, and then click Select.

   The new image appears on your draft page.

7. Click the Publish button in the toolbar to save the new image to the server.

EDITING IMAGES

Working with Flash Content

You can add Macromedia Flash movies to your Contribute pages as easily as you add any other image. When you insert a Flash file into a page, Contribute uploads a copy of the file to the server when you publish the page, just as it does with image files. You can also resize Flash files, or change their properties.

To insert a Flash file:

1. In Edit mode, put the insertion point where you want the Flash movie to appear.

2. Choose Insert > Flash Movie.
   The Select File dialog appears.

3. Navigate to the Flash file you want, select it, and then click the Select button.
   The Flash movie appears in your document. It may be represented by a placeholder with the Flash icon (**Figure 5.16**). Sometimes a still frame of the movie, called the *poster frame* will appear.

When used with some Web sites, Contribute doesn't show the content of the Flash file while you're editing the page. When this occurs, you must publish the page and view it in Contribute's browser (or an external Web browser) to see the full effect of the Flash movie on your page.

Figure 5.16 In Edit mode, some Flash movies may appear as placeholders; in which case you can't see the content.

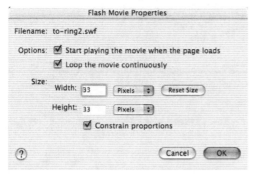

Figure 5.17 Use the Flash Movie Properties dialog to resize Flash content, as well as adjust the Flash movie's playback parameters.

To resize a Flash file:

1. In Edit mode, select the Flash movie you want to resize.

2. Drag one of the selection handles at the edges of the movie.

   or

   Choose Format > Flash Movie Properties. The Flash Movie Properties dialog opens (**Figure 5.17**).

3. In the Size area of the dialog, type the width and height you want for the movie.

   You can choose either Pixels or Percent from the Units pop-up menus.

4. (Optional) The "Constrain proportions" option is selected by default. If you want to resize the movie asymmetrically, uncheck this option.

5. Click OK.

✔ Tips

- If you don't like the new size of the movie, you can reopen the Flash Movie Properties dialog and click the Reset Size button to return the movie to its original size.

- The Flash Movie Properties dialog gives you more control over resizing movies than dragging does, since you can enter an exact size. It is also the only way to specify that the movie should take up a given percentage of the page's width and height.

To change a Flash file's properties:

1. In Edit mode, select the movie and choose Format > Flash Movie Properties. The Flash Movie Properties dialog opens.

2. Choose one or both of the two options (both are selected by default).

3. Click OK.

✔ Tips

- If you attempt to view a Flash movie in the Contribute browser and you haven't previously installed the free Macromedia Flash Player plug-in, Contribute prompts you to install it. Installing the player will also make the Flash Player available when you use Internet Explorer on either Windows or Mac, and Safari on the Mac.

- If Contribute crashes when you're editing Web pages containing Flash movies, update to the latest version of the Macromedia Flash Player MX, available from the Macromedia Web site (www.macromedia.com/downloads/).

- Contribute does not have an easy way to add media files other than Flash animations to your pages. You can add links to your pages that point to media files, such as MP3, WAV, Windows Media, or QuickTime files, and Contribute uploads those files to your server, but you won't be able to control their properties, preview, or play them in Contribute. If you need to use other kinds of media files in your pages, you should use a full-featured Web creation program, such as Dreamweaver MX.

- The name of the Flash file appears in the Flash Movie Properties dialog.

WORKING WITH LINKS

6

Hyperlinks, or more commonly just called *links*, are the lifeblood of Web pages, and Macromedia Contribute gives you a rich set of tools you can use to link to the Web pages on your site, Web addresses of pages on other sites, email addresses, non-HTML files on your Web server, and more. Contribute can create links from text or graphics on the pages you are editing to any of the preceding destinations.

Links consist of two parts: the text or image (sometimes called the *hot spot)* that the user of your Web page sees and clicks; and the *URL*, or Uniform Resource Locator, which is the address that tells the browser where to go to follow the link.

In this chapter, you'll learn how to use Contribute to handle all of your hyperlinking needs, by creating and editing links that will connect your Web pages to other pages on your site, or to the rest of the world.

About Linking

Contribute can create hyperlinks to any content it can browse to, whether the content is a file on your computer, a page that's been published on your Web site, a page that's still in draft form, or documents elsewhere on the Web. Note that what you link to doesn't necessarily have to be a Web page; the link can go to a downloadable file, a media clip such as a movie or Flash animation, or an image.

You use two kinds of links in Contribute:

◆ **Absolute links** include the entire URL to the page, such as `http://www.negrino.com/pages/books.html`. Absolute links usually point to a page not on the site containing the current page. When you create a link in Contribute to a page that's outside of the current site, Contribute always uses an absolute link.

◆ **Relative links** include just a part of the URL and point to a document within the current site. In the preceding example, a relative link to the page from another page on the same site would be `books.html`. Contribute automatically creates relative links when you link to a page within the current site.

The good news about using Contribute to create links is that you don't have to worry about the kind of link you're using, because Contribute automatically creates the kind of link that's best in a particular situation.

✔ Tip

■ To control the colors of links on your pages, choose Format > Page Properties, or press Ctrl-J (Cmd-J) while you're editing a page. In the Page Properties dialog, you can specify the link color, the visited-link color, and the active-link color. If these options are not available in the Page Properties dialog, it's probably because you're editing a page based on a template or you've been restricted to text-only page editing by your administrator. For more information, see "Setting Page Properties" in Chapter 3.

Figure 6.1 The Insert Link dialog allows you to link to draft pages you've created in Contribute but haven't yet published.

Linking to Draft Pages

Contribute makes links to pages that are in the editing process differently from the way it makes links to pages that have already been created and published. If you think about it for a moment, this makes perfect sense; you can't use Contribute's built-in browser to browse to and edit pages that Contribute hasn't yet published, because they don't have a Web address to browse to yet. So Contribute gives you a way to link to the pages it knows about, even though they've yet to officially appear on your site. Of course, you can also use Contribute to make links to pages that are already live on your site; see "Linking to Web Addresses," later in this chapter.

In terms of linking, Contribute treats a new page that is not yet saved or published the same as if it were a draft page.

To create a link to a new or draft page on your site:

1. Select the text or image you want to make into a link.

2. Choose Insert > Link > Drafts and Recent Pages, or press Ctrl-Alt-L (Cmd-Opt-L).

   or

   In the toolbar, click the Link pop-up menu, and choose Drafts and Recent Pages.

   or

   Right-click (Ctrl-click) the selected text or image, and choose Insert Link from the shortcut menu.

   The Insert Link dialog appears, with the Drafts and Recent Pages button already selected (**Figure 6.1**).

   The selected text appears in the "Link text" field of the dialog (if you're linking to an image, the "Link text" field doesn't appear). The new or draft pages that are available to you appear in the list.

continues on next page

3. Select one of the pages in the list.

A thumbnail of the page appears in the Preview section of the dialog.

4. (Optional) Click the Advanced button to expand the Insert Link dialog and make any changes to the options in that section (**Figure 6.2**).

To change the address of the page that's being linked to, modify the contents of the HREF field.

If the page to which you want to point the link has section anchors, they will appear in the "Section anchor" pop-up menu, and you can select the anchor there. You can find more information about section anchors in the "Adding and Editing Anchors" section of this chapter.

To have the clicked link open a new window, select New Window from the "Target frame" pop-up menu.

5. Click OK to create the link to the selected page.

✔ Tips

■ Contribute automatically fills in the HREF field in the Advanced section of the Insert Link dialog when you select the draft page for the link, basing the HREF on the name of that page. When you change the contents of the HREF field, you change the link destination, and Contribute won't link to the page you selected. The main benefit of the HREF field is to tell you the actual name of the page as that file will appear on the Web server; the name of the page in Figure 6.2 is the page title.

■ When you click the Advanced button, Contribute scans the selected page for section anchors, which appear in the "Section anchor" pop-up menu. When the page contains no anchors, you see <No anchors found> in the pop-up menu.

Figure 6.2 The Advanced section of the Insert Link dialog lets you target the destination of your link.

Setting Page Targets

In the "Target frame" pop-up menu in the Advanced section of the Insert Link dialog, you can select which browser frame, or *target*, displays when someone clicks the link. When the page you're linking to contains named frames, Contribute displays the frame names in the pop-up menu. Besides these named frames, you'll have three options (which also appear when the page you're linking to has no named frames). Many Contribute users are familiar with Dreamweaver, yet the two programs use different terminology for the same actions (Contribute tries to be more user-friendly and less code-oriented). I've included the Dreamweaver equivalent for the three target options. Not surprisingly, the Dreamweaver equivalent is also the entry that would need to be in the `target=` portion of the Anchor `HTML` tag—the tag that creates links.

- **Default** opens the new page in the same frame as the current page. The Dreamweaver equivalent is `_self`.

- **Entire window** replaces the frameset with the linked page. The Dreamweaver equivalent target is `_top`.

- **New window** loads the linked page in a new browser window. In Dreamweaver, the equivalent target is `_blank`. Use this option when the page you're linking to doesn't have frames; it allows you to easily open new windows with links.

LINKING TO DRAFT PAGES

Creating New Pages from Links

When you're adding to a site, you often want to create a link to a new page on the site. Contribute allows you to make the link and create the new page in one operation. Although you can create new pages on your site using Contribute's New Page command, creating pages and links simultaneously is easier than creating pages and then linking them later.

To create a new page from a link:

1. Select the text or image you want to make into a link.

2. Choose Insert > Link > Create New Page.

or

In the toolbar, click the Link pop-up menu and choose Create New Page.

or

Right-click (Ctrl-click) the selected text or image, and choose Insert Link from the shortcut menu.

The Insert Link dialog appears. If you used the menu bar or the toolbar to bring up this dialog, the New Page button will already be selected (**Figure 6.3**). If you used the shortcut menu, you'll need to click the Create New Page button in the dialog (on the Mac, the button is named New Page). By default, Contribute selects the Blank Web Page option.

Figure 6.3 In the Insert Link dialog, you can create a blank new page, or you can base the new page on sample pages or templates.

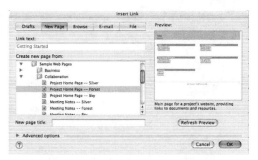

Figure 6.4 The Sample Web Pages folder contains a variety of generic but serviceable canned pages you can use as a jumping-off point for your own modifications.

Figure 6.5 Templates are custom pages created in Dreamweaver that you can use to create new pages in Contribute.

3. If you want to create a new blank page in your site, go to step 4.

   If you want the new page to be based on one of the Sample Pages, click the plus button (Windows) or the disclosure triangle (Mac) next to the Sample Web Pages folder to disclose its contents, and then choose the page you want (**Figure 6.4**).

   If you want the new page to be based on one of the Templates, click the plus button (Windows) or the disclosure triangle (Mac) next to the Templates folder to disclose its contents, and then choose the template you want to use (**Figure 6.5**). The site administrator designates these templates.

4. In the "New page title" field, type the title of the page as you want it to appear in a Web browser.

   The page title is the text that appears at the very top of the browser window, and it is the text used when the page is bookmarked.

5. (Optional) If you want the new page to open in a new browser window when the user clicks the link, click the Advanced button in the Insert Link dialog, and select New Window from the Target frame pop-up menu.

6. Click OK to create the link and the new page.

   Contribute creates and displays the new draft page, ready for you to edit and publish.

✔ Tips

- If the Sample Pages or Templates options are missing from the Insert Link dialog, your site administrator may have disabled these features for you. Check with your site administrator if you're unsure. See Chapter 10, "Site Administration," for more information about administering Contribute sites.

- If you selected an image for your link, the "Link text" field will not appear in the Insert Link dialog.

CREATING NEW PAGES FROM LINKS

Linking to Web Addresses

When you want to link to other Web pages, either ones that are already published on your site or elsewhere on the Web, you use the Browse to Web Page option in the Contribute Insert Link dialog.

It's helpful if you know the URL of the page you want to link to, but if you don't, no worries—you can use Contribute's built-in browser to find the page you want.

To link to a Web address:

1. Select the text or image you want to make into a link.

2. Choose Insert > Link > Browse to Web Page.

   or

   Choose Browse to Web Page from the Link pop-up menu in the toolbar.

   The Insert Link dialog opens (**Figure 6.6**).

3. In the Web address (URL) field, type the URL of the page you want to link to.

   or

   If you don't know the URL, click the Browse button, use the Browse to Link dialog to browse to the page you want to link to (**Figure 6.7**), and, when Contribute displays the page you want, click OK.

   Contribute displays the target page for the link in the Preview section of the Insert Link dialog and the URL in the Web address (URL) field.

4. Click OK to create the link.

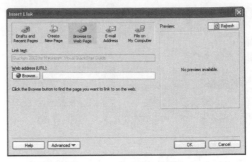

Figure 6.6 You can link to Web pages external to your site by browsing to the destination Web page.

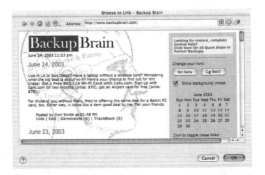

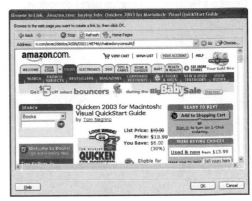

Figure 6.7 The Browse to Link dialog is actually a miniature Web browser. The Mac OS X version (top) and the Windows version (bottom) look a bit different but work virtually identically.

✔ Tips

- The Browse to Link window is resizable on Windows computers; you can adjust its size as you would any other window, by dragging an edge of the window. On the Mac, you can't resize the window.

- You don't have to link just to other Web pages. You can link to any content with a URL, including file downloads via FTP; media files such as Flash, QuickTime, or Windows Media movies; or anything else. Just type the URL of the item you want to link to in the "Web address (URL)" field.

- Don't forget that you can copy URLs from your standalone Web browser, such as Internet Explorer (Windows or Mac) or Safari (Mac), and paste them into the "Web address (URL)" field. Copying and pasting URLs is often faster than browsing to the target page.

- If necessary, you can edit the URL in either the "Web address (URL)" field or the HREF field that's displayed when you click the Advanced button at the bottom of the Insert Link dialog.

LINKING TO WEB ADDRESSES

Creating Email Links

When a user clicks a link to an email address on a Web page, the Web browser passes the request to an email program, which creates a new outgoing message with that address. Once again, use the Insert Link dialog to create an email address link.

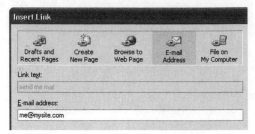

Figure 6.8 Type the destination email address to create an email link.

To create an email link:

1. Select the text or image you want to make into a link.

2. Choose Insert > Link > E-mail Address.

   or

   Choose E-mail Address from the Link pop-up menu in the toolbar.

   The Insert Link dialog opens, with the selected text already inserted in the "Link text" field (**Figure 6.8**).

3. In the "E-mail address" field, type the address. Click OK.

✔ Tip

■ Clicking the Advanced button in the Insert Link dialog shows you the full email address link in its HTML form—that is, `mailto:me@myaddress.com`. Because `mailto` links open email programs, not other Web pages, Contribute disables the "Section anchor" and "Target frame" pop-up menus.

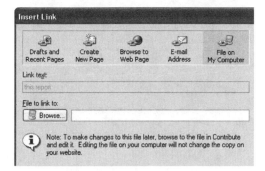

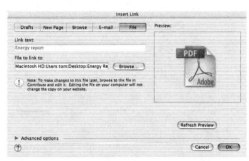

Figure 6.9 You can link to files on your computer when you choose File on My Computer (Windows, top) or click the File button in the Insert Link dialog (Mac, bottom).

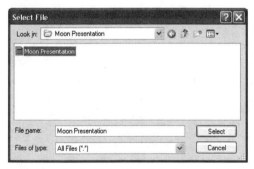

Figure 6.10 Use the Select File dialog to navigate to the file you want to upload to your Web site.

Linking to Local Files

Contribute lets you link to a document that resides on your local hard drive or to documents that reside on network disks that are connected to your computer. For example, you can make a link to a local text or image file, a Word file, or a PDF document. When you publish the page that contains the link, Contribute uploads a copy of the document to your Web site, where it resides in the same directory as the HTML pages on your site. When users click the link on your Web site, their browser downloads a copy of the file.

You use this linking method to create links to items you want users of your Web site to be able to download.

To link to files on your computer or network:

1. Select the text or image you want to make into a link.

2. Choose Insert > Link > File on My Computer.

   or

   Choose File on My Computer from the Link pop-up menu in the toolbar.

   The Insert Link dialog opens, with the selected text already inserted in the "Link text" field (**Figure 6.9**).

3. Click the Browse button.

   The Select File dialog appears (**Figure 6.10**).

continues on next page

4. Navigate to the file you want to upload and link to, select the file, and click the Select button.

   If the file resides on a network volume, Contribute may ask you to save a copy of the file on your local hard drive.

   If the File Download or Save As dialog appears, click Save and save a copy of the file on your hard drive.

5. Click OK to close the Insert Link dialog.

   Contribute displays a dialog that reminds you that it will make a copy of the file on your Web site, and that in order to edit the file, you need to edit the copy on your Web site with Contribute's help, not the one on your computer (**Figure 6.11**).

6. Click OK.

   When you publish the page, Contribute uploads a copy of the file to your Web site.

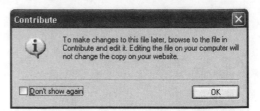

Figure 6.11 After you upload the file, Contribute reminds you that you need to edit the copy of the file on your Web site, not the one on your computer.

✔ Tip

- When the name of the file you're uploading contains any special characters, including ampersand, comma, slash, hyphen, asterisk, number sign, or some others, Contribute displays an alert dialog letting you know that some Web servers won't access the files properly. You should eliminate the special characters from the filename before you upload the file.

Figure 6.12 Type the section anchor name.

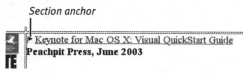

Figure 6.13 The section anchor icon appears only in the Contribute Edit mode.

Adding and Editing Anchors

A *section anchor* (sometimes called a *named anchor*) is a link to a specific location on a Web page. Whereas regular links point to an entire document, section anchors link to a place in the document. You use section anchors when you want to direct visitors to a specific place within a long page rather than to the top of the page.

Working with anchors has two steps: First, you need to name the part of the page where you want to link, which creates the anchor. Then you need to link to the anchor from another page.

To add a section anchor:

1. On the page where you want the anchor, click to place the insertion point at the anchor point, or select the text or image to which you want the anchor to be attached.

    This will be the destination of the anchor.

2. Choose Insert > Section Anchor, or press Ctrl-Alt-A (Cmd-Opt-A).

    The Section Anchor dialog appears.

3. Type the name you want for the section anchor (**Figure 6.12**).

    The section anchor name cannot start with a number and cannot have spaces, so I recommend that you use a single, lowercase word, followed by a number, for the name.

4. Click OK.

    A small flag icon appears at the anchor point on the Web page (**Figure 6.13**). This icon appears only when you are in Edit mode in Contribute. The flag icon does not appear when you're in Contribute's Browse mode, or when visitors are viewing the page on the Web.

✔ Tip

■ If you can't see the section anchor flag icons in Edit mode, you might need to adjust one of the Contribute Preferences. Choose Edit > Preferences (Contribute > Preferences), and then select the Invisible Elements category. Make sure you have the "Show Section Anchors When Editing a Page" option selected, and then click OK.

ADDING AND EDITING ANCHORS

To link to a section anchor:

1. Browse to the page from which you want to link to the page that contains the anchors.

2. Select the text or image you want to make into a link to the section anchor.

3. Choose Insert > Link > Browse to Web Page.
   or
   Choose Browse to Web Page from the Link pop-up menu in the toolbar.
   The Insert Link dialog appears.

4. Click the Browse button.
   The Browse to Link dialog appears. This dialog is actually a Web browser and works like any other browser window.

5. Use the dialog to browse to the page you want to link to. When Contribute displays the page you want, click OK.
   The Web address of the page you will be linking to appears in the "Web address (URL)" field of the Insert Link dialog (**Figure 6.14**).

6. Click the Advanced button to expand the dialog.

7. From the "Section anchor" pop-up menu, select the anchor you want to use (**Figure 6.15**).

8. Click OK.

✔ Tip

■ If the page that contains the anchor is on one of your draft pages, choose Insert > Link > Drafts and Recent Pages in Step 3.

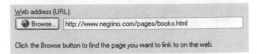

Figure 6.14 The page that contains the section anchors appears in the "Web address (URL)" field.

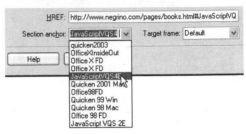

Figure 6.15 Select the anchor you want to use from the "Section anchor" pop-up menu.

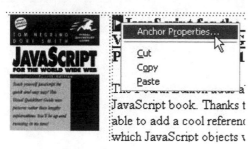

Figure 6.16 Edit the section anchor name by using Anchor Properties.

To modify an anchor:

1. Select the anchor on the page you're editing.

2. Right-click (Ctrl-click) the anchor's flag icon. The Anchor shortcut menu appears (**Figure 6.16**).

3. If you want to rename the anchor, choose Anchor Properties from the shortcut menu. The Edit Section Anchor dialog appears.

4. Change the name and then click OK.

✔ Tips

■ To delete an anchor, select its icon and press the Backspace or Delete key.

■ You can also cut, copy, or paste named anchors using the anchor shortcut menu.

Editing and Removing Links

A regular part of a site's maintenance is changing or deleting links. Contribute uses the Insert Link dialog to modify links as well as to create them.

To edit a link:

1. Browse to the page where you want to edit links, and click the Edit Page button.

2. Right-click (Ctrl-click) the link you want to edit. From the resulting shortcut menu, choose Link Properties.
   The Insert Link dialog opens.

3. Use the Browse button or the HREF field in the Advanced section of the Insert Link dialog to change the destination of the link.

4. Click OK.

To remove links:

1. Browse to the page where you want to edit links, and click the Edit Page button.

2. Right-click (Ctrl-click) the link you wish to edit. From the resulting shortcut menu, choose Remove Link.
   Contribute removes the link.

✔ Tip

- Contribute doesn't ask for confirmation before it removes a link. If you remove the wrong link, choose Edit > Undo or Ctrl-Z (Cmd-Z) to get the link.

CREATING TABLES

Top 10 U.S. Box Office As of October 2002			
Rank	Title	Cumulative Gross	Release Date
1	Titanic	$600,788,188	12/19/97
2	Star Wars	$460,998,007	5/25/77
3	E.T. The Extra-Terrestrial	$434,949,459	6/11/82
4	Star Wars: Episode I - The Phantom Menace	$431,088,295	5/19/99
5	Spider-Man	$405,692,151	5/3/02
6	Jurassic Park	$357,067,947	6/11/93
7	Forrest Gump	$329,694,499	7/6/94
8	Harry Potter and the Sorcerer's Stone	$317,557,891	11/16/01
9	Lord of the Rings: The Fellowship of the Ring	$313,364,114	12/19/01
10	The Lion King	$312,855,561	6/15/94

Figure 7.1 The HTML table format is perfect for tables with lots of data.

You will often use tables on Web pages to present *tabular information*—that is, data best presented in the form of rows and columns (**Figure 7.1**). But tables are also useful as layout devices to help get around some of the limitations of HTML. Before tables were introduced for layout purposes, text and images were left-aligned on Web pages, and there was not a good way to arrange page elements.

When you use a table to lay out the elements of your Web page, you can put images next to text without worrying about the text's wrapping oddly around the image; create columns of text; and position different type treatments, such as headlines, body text, and figure captions, more precisely.

Macromedia Contribute lets you create tables on your Web pages (unless, of course, your site administrator has disallowed their use), and tables will probably be an important part of the way you add content to your site. In this chapter, you'll learn how to use and format tables, ensure that tables and their content look the way you intend, and save time when you're using tables.

Creating a New Table

Tables typically consist of one or more rows and one or more columns. Each rectangular area at the intersection of a row and column is called a *cell*. Cells contain the page's text or images, and items within a cell can't extend past the cell's boundaries.

You can insert a table anywhere on a page, even within another table (this is called *nesting*). By default, Contribute creates tables with three rows and three columns, but you can easily change that format during the process of inserting the table.

If you can't create a table, your site administrator may have disabled this function. Check with the administrator if you have problems. If you're using a Macromedia Dreamweaver template as the basis of your page, you may not need to insert tables at all; the site designer may have created one or more editable areas in the template, which you fill with text or images. Designers often put editable areas inside tables they create; the Contribute user can't modify the table, which is being used as a layout device, but he or she can add to and edit editable areas within tables.

To add a table to your page:

1. Browse to and edit the page where you want to insert a table.

2. Place the insertion point where you want the table to appear.

3. Click the Insert Table button on the toolbar.

   or

   Choose Table > Insert > Table, or press Ctrl-Alt-T (Cmd-Opt-T).

   The Insert Table dialog appears (**Figure 7.2**).

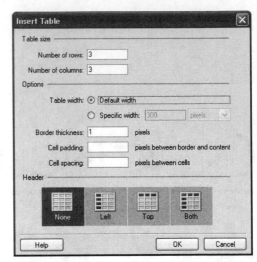

Figure 7.2 Get started building a table with the Insert Table dialog.

Figure 7.3 You can set the width of your table either in pixels or as a percentage of the browser page width.

✔ Tips

- If you're not sure how you want to use tables to lay out your page's elements, consider sketching out a map showing where things will go. It's usually easier to have a plan before you start creating tables and entering content.

- To insert a table within a table, enter Edit mode, place the insertion point inside an existing table, and click the Table button on the toolbar. Nested tables offer even greater layout flexibility.

- You don't have to get the number of rows and columns right the first time; you can always add or subtract them later. See the sections "Inserting Rows and Columns" and "Deleting Table Elements" later in this chapter.

4. Enter the number of rows you want in the table, and press Tab.

5. Enter the number of columns you want in the table.

6. Choose how you want to define the table's width (**Figure 7.3**). Selecting "Default width" creates a table with columns that are 200 pixels wide. If you want a different table width, select "Specific width," and then enter a number in the text box. Choose the units (either pixels or percent of the page width) of the width you enter using the pop-up menu to the right of the text box.

7. Set one or more (or none) of the following (see the "Table Anatomy" sidebar for explanations of these settings):
   - ▲ Enter a figure in the "Border thickness" text box for the size of the border, in pixels, that will be displayed between cells.
   - ▲ Enter a figure in the "Cell padding" text box for the amount of space, in pixels, between the content and the cell border.
   - ▲ Enter a figure in the "Cell spacing" text box for the number of pixels of space between cells.

8. Choose the kind of header you want: None, Left, Top, or Both. The icons for the headers show you what each choice looks like.

9. Click OK.
   The table appears in your draft page.

Table Anatomy

Besides rows and columns, tables have several other attributes that affect how they look:

Border thickness is the width of the border around the table, in pixels (**Figure 7.4**). Contribute sets it to zero by default, which results in no border. If the border thickness is set to a nonzero amount, you will also see a border between table cells. You set the border thickness to zero when you're using tables for page layout.

Cell padding is the amount of space, in pixels, between a cell's borders and its content (**Figure 7.5**). Use this setting to give cell content more breathing room within cells.

Cell spacing is the amount of space between each table cell, also measured in pixels (**Figure 7.6**). Wide cell spacing gives the table a look that is very 1996, so use this setting with care.

Border color is the color of the border around the table and between the table's cells.

Background color is the color of the cell's contents (though you can set the color of text in the cell separately). You can also use the Text Color attributes to color text within the cell.

Table header tags part of the table as a header. The header is formatted as bold and centered, but more important, it has the `<th>` HTML tag, which allows screen readers used by visually disabled users to correctly read the table. It's better to use a table header tag in Contribute than to manually make cells bold and centered.

Sales Territory	1st Quarter (00)	2nd Quarter (00)
North	$2300	$2800
East	$5750	$5200
South	$3100	$3600
West	$8250	$7550

Sales Territory	1st Quarter (00)	2nd Quarter (00)
North	$2300	$2800
East	$5750	$5200
South	$3100	$3600
West	$8250	$7550

Sales Territory	1st Quarter (00)	2nd Quarter (00)
North	$2300	$2800
East	$5750	$5200
South	$3100	$3600
West	$8250	$7550

Figure 7.4 The same table with a border thickness of zero pixels (top), 1 pixel (middle), and 10 pixels (bottom). Cell padding and cell spacing are set to zero.

Sales Territory	1st Quarter (00)	2nd Quarter (00)
North	$2300	$2800
East	$5750	$5200
South	$3100	$3600
West	$8250	$7550

Figure 7.5 Cell padding has been set to 5 pixels, which gives more air around the table contents.

Sales Territory	1st Quarter (00)	2nd Quarter (00)
North	$2300	$2800
East	$5750	$5200
South	$3100	$3600
West	$8250	$7550

Figure 7.6 Cell spacing of 5 pixels gives wide borders between cells—a dated look. The border is emphasized with a color to make it easier to see.

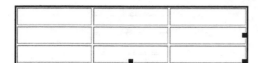

Figure 7.7 This table is selected. Around its edges it has a thick border with resize handles.

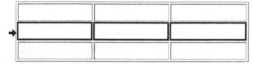

Figure 7.8 When the pointer changes to an arrow, the whole row can be selected.

Selecting table elements

To work effectively with a table, you'll need to know how to select its elements. You can select an entire table; one or more rows and columns; an individual cell or multiple cells; and nonadjacent cells, rows, or columns.

To select the entire table:

◆ Click the bottom or the right edge of the table.

or

Click the table's upper-left corner.

or

Click in the table, and then choose Table > Select Table; or press Ctrl-T (Cmd-T).

A border with resize handles appears around the table (**Figure 7.7**).

✔ Tip

■ Right-clicking (Ctrl-clicking) any interior cell border also selects the entire table.

To select an entire row:

1. Place the pointer at the left edge of a row. The pointer becomes an arrow.

2. Click to select the entire row (**Figure 7.8**). You can click and drag to select multiple rows.

To select an entire column:

1. Place the pointer at the top edge of a column.

   The pointer becomes an arrow.

2. Click to select the entire column (**Figure 7.9**).

   You can click and drag to select multiple columns.

To select a single cell:

◆ Click and drag in the cell.

   or

   Click in the cell, then choose Edit > Select All, or press Ctrl-A (Cmd-A).

   or

   Triple click inside the cell.

To select multiple adjacent cells:

◆ Click in the first cell you want to select, and drag to the last cell.

   or

   Click in the first cell you want to select, hold down Shift, and then click in the last cell. You can also Shift-click in this manner to select rows or columns.

To select nonadjacent cells:

◆ Click in the first cell, hold down Ctrl (Cmd), and then click the other cells you want to select (**Figure 7.10**). You can also Ctrl-click (Cmd-click) to select rows or columns.

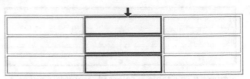

Figure 7.9 The pointer also changes to an arrow when you select columns.

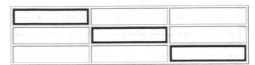

Figure 7.10 By Ctrl-clicking (Cmd-clicking), you can select nonadjacent cells.

CREATING A NEW TABLE

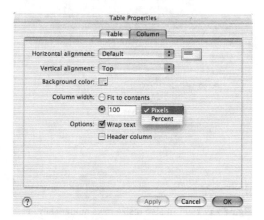

Figure 7.11 You can resize columns numerically in the Table Properties dialog.

Resizing table elements

You can resize tables horizontally or vertically, and also make columns wider and rows taller.

To resize an entire table:

1. Click the bottom or the right edge of the table. The table is selected, and a border with resize handles appears around it.

2. Drag one of the resize handles. To widen the table, drag the handle on the right edge of the table; to make the table taller, drag the handle on the bottom edge of the table; and to make the table grow in both directions simultaneously, drag the handle at the bottom-right corner of the table. Holding down the Shift key as you drag will maintain the proportions of the table.

To resize columns:

1. Select the column you want to resize.

2. Drag the column's right border.

   or

   Click the Table button on the toolbar. The Table Properties dialog appears, with the Column tab selected (**Figure 7.11**). Type a number in the "Column width" text box, and then choose either pixels or percent for the units from the pop-up menu. Alternatively, select "Fit to contents"; this makes the column resize to fit the contents.

CREATING A NEW TABLE

To resize rows:

1. Select the row you want to resize.

2. Drag the bottom border of the row.

   or

   Click the Table button on the toolbar. The Table Properties dialog appears, with the Row tab selected (**Figure 7.12**). Enter a number in pixels in the "Row height" text box, or click "Fit to contents," which makes the row resize to fit the contents.

✔ Tips

- If you set a width in percentage for a table, the table resizes based on the width of the user's browser window. This may really change the layout of your site. You should make sure that you preview the layout in a separate browser and resize the browser window to see the effect.

- Tables always stretch to fit the content inside the table.

- Text inside cells usually wraps to fit the width of the cell. To force the cell to expand to the width of the text, you can turn off text wrapping on a cell-by-cell basis. Ctrl-click in the cell, and then choose Table Cell Properties from the shortcut menu. Unselect the box next to "Wrap text," then click OK.

- Don't be misled into thinking you have ultimate control over row heights and column widths, and therefore control over what your site visitor sees. Different browsers display content differently, and short of previewing your site with every browser ever made on every computer platform, there's no way to be absolutely certain that your site visitor will see exactly what you intended.

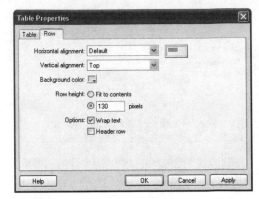

Figure 7.12 You can also resize rows numerically in the Table Properties dialog.

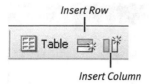

Insert Row

田 Table 📑 🗓

Insert Column

Figure 7.13 You can insert rows and columns quickly with the toolbar buttons.

Comedies	Tragedies
As You Like It	Hamlet
The Tempest	King Lear

Comedies	Tragedies
As You Like It	Hamlet
The Tempest	King Lear

Figure 7.14 A row has been selected in this table (top), and then a new row has been inserted above it (bottom).

Inserting Rows and Columns

Contribute allows you to add rows or columns to your table either singly or in multiples.

To insert a single row in a table:

1. Place the insertion point in a table cell.

2. Click the Insert Row button in the toolbar (**Figure 7.13**). A new row will appear below the row where the insertion point is.

   or

   Choose Table > Insert > Insert Row Above, or press Ctrl-M (Cmd-M).

   or

   Choose Table > Insert > Insert Row Below.

   or

   Right-click (Ctrl-click) in the cell, and choose either Insert Row Above or Insert Row Below from the shortcut menu.

   The row appears in your table (**Figure 7.14**).

✔ Tip

■ If the insertion point is in the last cell of the table, pressing Tab adds a row to the bottom of the table.

To insert a single column in a table:

1. Place the insertion point in a table cell.

2. Click the Insert Column button in the toolbar. A new column will appear to the right of the insertion point.

   or

   Choose Table > Insert > Insert Column to the Left.

   or

   Choose Table > Insert > Insert Column to the Right.

   or

   Right-click (Ctrl-click) in the cell, and from the shortcut menu choose either Insert Column to the Left or Insert Column to the Right.

   The column appears in your table.

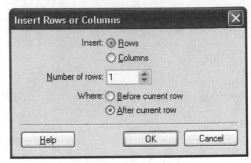

Figure 7.15 The Insert Rows or Columns dialog allows you to add multiple rows or columns in one operation.

To insert multiple rows or columns into a table:

1. Place the insertion point in a table cell.

2. Right-click, and then choose Insert Multiple Rows or Columns from the shortcut menu.

   or

   Choose Table > Insert > Multiple Rows or Columns.

   The Insert Rows or Columns dialog appears (**Figure 7.15**).

3. Select either the Rows or Columns radio button.

4. Enter the number of rows or columns you want to add. You can either type a number into the text box, or use the arrow buttons next to the text box to increase or decrease the number.

5. Click the appropriate button to select the location of the new rows or columns.

   The rows or columns appear in your table.

Deleting Table Elements

If you want to remove tables, rows, or columns, you can make short work of the task.

To delete a table:

1. Select the table by clicking its right or bottom edge. A border with resize handles appears around the table.

2. Press Backspace (Delete).

To delete rows:

1. Select one or more rows.

2. Press Backspace (Delete).

   or

   Choose Table > Delete > Row.

   or

   Right-click the row, and then choose Delete Row from the shortcut menu.

   The row disappears from the table.

To delete columns:

1. Select one or more columns.

2. Press Backspace (Delete).

   or

   Choose Table > Delete > Column.

   or

   Right-click the row, and then choose Delete Column from the shortcut menu.

   The columns disappear from the table.

Formatting Tables

Contribute comes with 17 preset table formats, which apply fonts, cell borders, and cell-background colors to tables to provide a more attractive look (**Figure 7.16**). They are similar to features of Microsoft Excel's AutoFormat option for worksheets.

To apply table formatting:

1. Place the insertion point inside the table you want to format.

2. Choose Table > Format Table.
   The Format Table dialog appears (**Figure 7.17**).

3. From the Format list on the Basic tab, choose a format.
   A sample of the format appears in the dialog.

4. Click OK.
   The format is applied to the table (**Figure 7.18**).

✔ Tip

■ The preset formats only work on one table at a time. If you have nested tables, you'll need to apply a preset format to each table separately.

Sales Territory	1st Quarter (00)	2nd Quarter (00)
North	$2300	$2800
East	$5750	$5200
South	$3100	$3600
West	$8250	$7550

Figure 7.16 Using contrasting colors in rows (one of Contribute's preset table formats) can often make tables more readable.

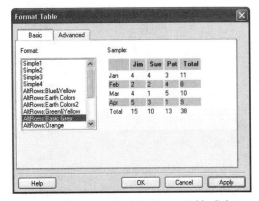

Figure 7.17 The Basic tab of the Format Table dialog gives you 17 preset table formats.

Recipient	Gift	Purchased?
Sean	Playstation 2, games	No
Rachel	DVD player	Yes
Aaron	PS2 games	No
Brandy	Clothes gift certificate	Yes
Sierra	Gardening things	No
Robert	Educational software	No
Kayla	Doll house	Yes
Trinity	Toddler toys	No
Sophia	Baby toys	Yes

Figure 7.18 The preset format is applied to the table.

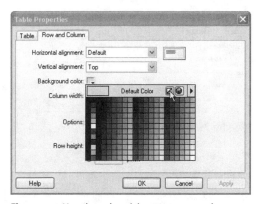

Figure 7.19 Use the color picker to remove colors as well as to apply them.

To remove the background colors from a table:

1. Select the table's cells (be sure not to select the whole table).

2. Right-click (Ctrl-click), and choose Table Cell Properties from the shortcut menu.

   The Table Properties dialog appears, set to the Row and Column tab.

3. Click in the color box next to "Background color."

   The color picker appears (**Figure 7.19**).

4. At the top of the color picker, click the Default Color box (the square with a red slash through it).

5. Click OK.

   Contribute removes the background colors from the selected table cells.

Saving Page Elements for Later Use

You can't create and save a custom table format in the Format Table dialog, but you can certainly create, format, and save an empty table for later use. This technique is also useful for saving other page elements you may want to use on more than one page.

First, create a new page on your site. On the new page, create a table, and then customize it with the Format Table dialog. Publish the page but don't link it to any other page on your site; that way, site visitors won't accidentally stumble upon it. When Contribute publishes the page, it switches back to the browser and displays the page with the formatted table. Finally, choose Bookmarks > Add Bookmark.

When you need to use the that table style again, use the bookmark to go to the page with the table, click Edit Page to create a draft of that page, copy the table, switch to the draft page where you want to use the table, and paste it in.

Custom table formatting

Contribute lets you create your own custom table formatting, although unfortunately you can't name and save the custom format for later use from the Format Table dialog. The Advanced tab of the Format Table dialog gives you the control you need to quickly create and apply a custom table format.

To apply custom table formatting:

1. Place the insertion point inside the table you want to format.

2. Choose Table > Format Table.
   The Format Table dialog appears.

3. Select the Advanced tab (**Figure 7.20**).

4. Under "Table Properties," enter a number for the border width. If you don't want a border, enter 0.

5. In the "Left column" section, choose a text alignment and a text style from the pop-up menus.

6. Under "Header row," make any changes to the background color, text color, text alignment, and text style.

7. In the "Other rows" section, choose the row color. This will be your main row color.

8. From the "Alternate row" pop-up menu, choose how often you want alternate rows to be colored. Your choices are to not alternate, or alternate every other, every two, every three, or every four rows.

9. Choose from the Color pop-up menu for the alternate row color.

10. Click OK.
    Contribute applies the new formatting to your table.

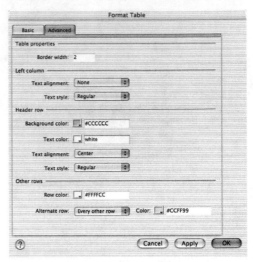

Figure 7.20 You can use the Advanced tab of the Format Table dialog to create your own table formats.

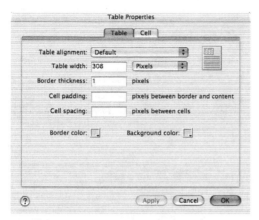

Figure 7.21 You can set the way text will wrap around your table in the "Table alignment" pop-up menu in the Table Properties dialog.

Setting Table Properties

Table properties apply to the entire table, and Contribute allows you to change the table's alignment and width, its border width and border color, its cell padding and cell spacing, and the background color for the whole table.

To set table properties:

1. Place the insertion point in the table you want to modify.

2. Choose Table > Table Properties, or press Ctrl-Shift-T (Cmd-Shift-T).

   or

   Right-click (Ctrl-click) in the table, and choose Table Properties from the short-cut menu.

   The Table Properties dialog appears (**Figure 7.21**).

continues on next page

Who's on Top: The Story of Formatting Precedence

Contribute allows you to set formatting for tables, rows, and cells separately, but some formatting is more important—here's the pecking order:

1. Cells

2. Rows

3. Table

Cell formatting takes precedence over row formatting, and row formatting takes precedence over table formatting. For example, if you set the background color for a single cell to green, then set the background color for the row that the cell is in to red, and then set the background color for the entire table to purple, neither the cell nor the row will change color, because their formatting preferences take precedence over those of the overall table formatting.

On occasion, you'll attempt to apply some sort of formatting to an entire table and it doesn't appear to work. Chances are, all the cells in the table had formatting applied to them at some time in the past, and because that cell formatting trumps the table formatting, the table format won't work until you change the cell formatting.

3. From the "Table alignment" pop-up menu choose Default, Left, Center, or Right.

Each alignment has a different effect, as shown in **Figure 7.22**. There are also icons in the Table Properties dialog that show how the table will be aligned with text.

4. Make any other changes you want.

5. Click OK to apply the changes to your table.

✔ Tip

■ When you align the table to the right, a small placeholder icon appears in the left margin (see the bottom example in Figure 7.22). This marks the beginning of the table on the page. The placeholder icon only appears on the draft page.

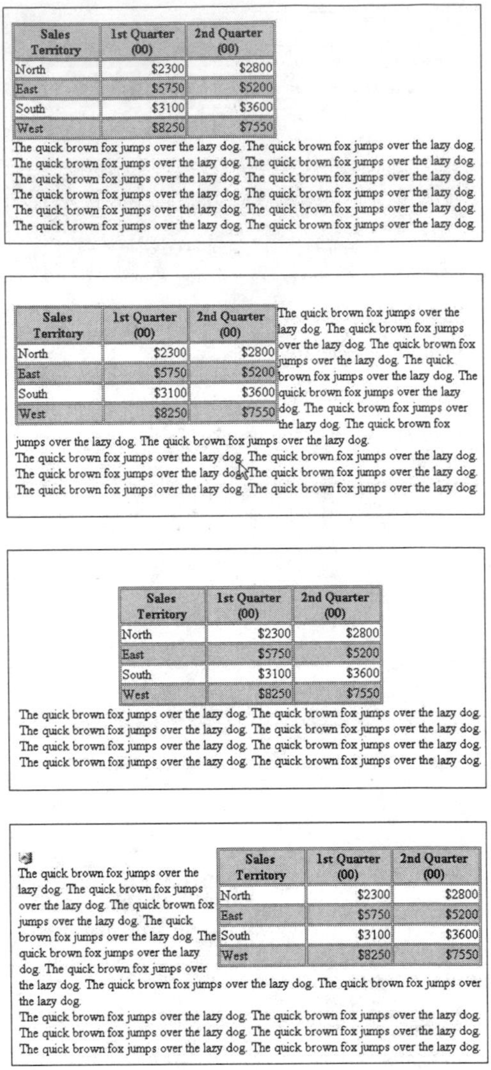

Figure 7.22 The effects of different types of table alignment, set in the Table Properties dialog. From top to bottom, Default, Left, Center, and Right alignments.

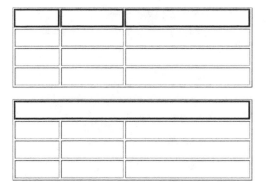

Figure 7.23 The three cells at the top of this table (top) have been merged into one (bottom).

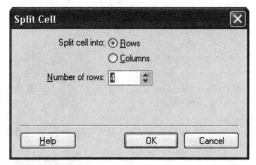

Figure 7.24 You can use the Split Cell dialog to divide cells into rows or columns.

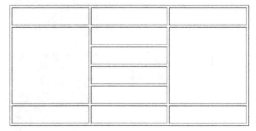

Figure 7.25 In this example, the center cell has been split into four cells.

Merging and Splitting Cells

Contribute lets you combine two or more adjacent cells into one larger cell, or split a single cell into two or more cells.

To merge cells:

1. Select the cells you want to merge.

2. Choose Table > Merge Cells, or press Ctrl-Alt-M (Cmd-Opt-M).

   or

   Right-click (Ctrl-click), and then choose Merge Cells from the shortcut menu.

   The cells merge (**Figure 7.23**).

✔ Tip

- You can merge an entire row or column into one cell.

To split cells:

1. Place the insertion point in the cell you want to split into two cells.

2. Choose Table > Split Cell, or press Ctrl-Alt-S (Cmd-Opt-S).

   or

   Right-click (Ctrl-click), and then choose Split Cell from the shortcut menu.

   The Split Cell dialog appears (**Figure 7.24**).

3. Choose whether to split the cell into rows or columns.

4. Enter the number of new rows or columns for the split.

5. Click OK.

   The cell divides into two or more cells (**Figure 7.25**).

✔ Tip

- Even if you select multiple cells, Contribute can split only one cell at a time.

MERGING AND SPLITTING CELLS

Setting Cell Properties

Cell properties apply to the content of a single cell. You can set the cell content's horizontal or vertical alignment, set the cell's background color, or set whether or not the text wraps within the cell.

To set cell properties:

1. Place the insertion point in the cell you want to format.

2. Choose Table > Table Cell Properties. The Table Properties dialog appears, with the Cell tab selected (**Figure 7.26**).

3. From the "Horizontal alignment" pop-up menu choose Left, Center, or Right (**Figure 7.27**).

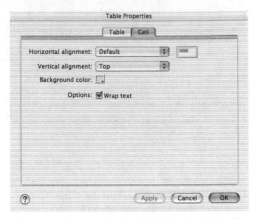

Figure 7.26 The second tab of the Table Properties dialog changes depending on what is selected. Because a cell was selected, the tab shows Table Cell Properties.

Figure 7.27 Horizontal text alignment within a cell. From top to bottom, Left, Center, and Right text alignment.

Figure 7.28 Vertical text alignment within a cell. From top to bottom, Top, Middle, and Bottom alignment.

4. From the "Vertical alignment" pop-up menu choose Top, Middle, or Bottom (**Figure 7.28**).

5. To change the cell's background color, click in the box next to "Background color" to bring up the color picker.

6. If you don't want the text in the cell to wrap, unselect the "Wrap text" check box.

7. Click OK to apply your cell formatting.

SETTING CELL PROPERTIES

Sorting Table Contents

It's not uncommon to enter data into a table, then add more data, and then want to sort the whole thing. You asked for it, Contribute can do it. The program sorts by any column in your table, either numerically or alphabetically, in ascending or descending order, and can sort on two successive criteria.

There are some limitations to Contribute's sorting abilities. You cannot sort merged cells, and Contribute doesn't have the ability to sort part of a table, so you can't, for example, have the program ignore the merged cells you used for your table's title. Contribute displays an error message if you try to sort a table containing merged cells.

Another problem is that the sorting algorithm Contribute uses isn't terribly smart. For example, you can sort numerically, but Contribute doesn't understand dates in tables, so you're liable to get sorts like this:

5/19/99

5/25/77

5/3/02

Contribute sorted the dates numerically, reading left to right, which resulted in an incorrect sort.

Despite these restrictions, table sorting in Contribute is useful—you just have to be aware of them.

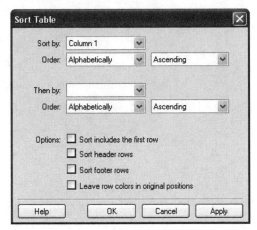

Figure 7.29 The Sort Table dialog lets you sort the contents of your table either alphabetically or numerically.

To sort a table:

1. Place the insertion point in any cell of the table you want to sort.

2. Choose Table > Sort Table.
   The Sort Table dialog appears (**Figure 7.29**).

3. From the "Sort by" pop-up menu choose the column you want to sort.

4. In the Order pop-up menu on the left, choose whether to sort the column alphabetically or numerically.

5. In the Order pop-up menu on the right, choose whether to sort the column in ascending or descending order.

6. If you want to sort on a second set of criteria repeat steps 3 through 5 with the "Then by" set of pop-up menus.

7. Make any selections from the Options list.
   By default, the "Sort includes the first row" option is *not* selected. This is because the first row of a table is frequently a header row. if your table doesn't seem to be sorting properly, check this option.

8. Click OK.
   Contribute sorts your table according to the criteria you selected.

✔ Tips

- Contribute can't sort on rows, just columns.

- If you want a merged row at the top of your table, do the sort first, and then merge the cells.

- Be careful when you're sorting numbers. If you accidentally leave the sort on Alphabetically, you'll get an alphanumeric sort (1, 10, 2, 20, 3, 30) instead of a numeric sort (1, 2, 3, 10, 20, 30).

SORTING TABLE CONTENTS

USING DREAMWEAVER TEMPLATES

Macromedia Contribute is in some ways a bit of a paradox. Now that Web sites have become complex, requiring the skills of highly trained designers and Web programmers, Contribute returns to the content contributor the ability to change Web sites simply and directly. With Contribute, you can add to existing Web sites, but you can't create new sites. Contribute is a terrific tool for the novice, but it works best when using page templates created with Macromedia Dreamweaver, a complex program for Web professionals. Dreamweaver templates let Contribute users add content to pages without bringing down the wrath of the site designer if a mistake is made, and the templates allow everyone, from the administrative assistant to the Web expert, to make quick changes to Web pages, knowing that the site will still look good and work well when they're finished.

In this chapter, you'll learn how to create new pages based on Dreamweaver templates, how templates can let you "fill in the blanks" without sacrificing good design, and how to create Sample Pages, the other kind of templates used in Contribute.

Creating New Pages from Dreamweaver Templates

Two kinds of templates are available to Contribute. The first are templates made in and saved from Dreamweaver, and are called, not surprisingly, *Dreamweaver templates*. The second kind, called *Sample Pages*, are Web pages made in other programs and saved for use in Contribute. For more information about using sample pages, see the "Building New Pages from Sample Pages" section in Chapter 3, or the section "Creating Sample Pages Templates" in Chapter 12, "Customizing Contribute."

A Dreamweaver template, which the site administrator places on the Web site, provides a prebuilt page layout and includes a variety of page elements that appear on all pages made from that template. The template gives you a starting point for new pages. For example, a template may have a navigation bar and places for images and headings, plus places for body text. The page designer can designate these body text areas as *editable regions*, meaning that you can change them in Contribute. Other places on the page, *locked regions*, are not editable; the navigation bar is an example of an element typically in a locked region. Locked regions make it possible for designers to create templates that are ready for you to add content and yet protect you from accidentally messing up the page design. When you put the pointer over one of the locked regions, it changes to the international symbol for "no" (the circle with a diagonal slash through it), and you cannot place the insertion point in the locked region. When you work on a page in Contribute based on a Dreamweaver template, most of the page is already done for you; all you need to do is fill in the content in the page's editable regions.

✔ Tips

■ You don't have to choose a template from the current Web site, though most of the time you'll want to do just that. You can instead choose a template in the New Page dialog from any of the sites for which you have a connection.

■ Dreamweaver templates must be created in Dreamweaver 4 or later to work with Contribute.

■ Contribute users can't create, delete, or edit Dreamweaver templates.

■ Though Contribute works best when you have a network connection, you can use templates to create pages when you work offline. Contribute uses copies of the site templates saved on your computer the last time you connected to the Web site. The program updates its copies of the templates and gets any new templates from the server upon startup or when you edit the site connection.

■ In most cases Contribute also works with templates created in Adobe GoLive 6.0, because they follow the same standard as Dreamweaver templates.

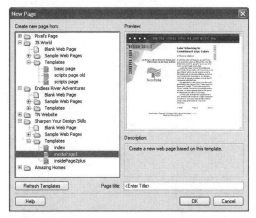

Figure 8.1 The New Page dialog's Preview pane helps you select the correct template.

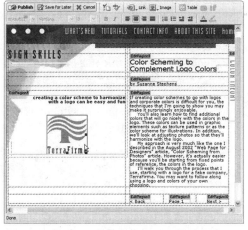

Figure 8.2 This new page contains a lot of information in the editable regions.

To create a page from a Dreamweaver template:

1. Browse to the Web site where you want a new page. It must be a site for which you have established a connection.

2. Click New Page on the toolbar.

   or

   Choose File > New Page, or press Ctrl-N (Cmd-N).

3. In the New Page dialog, click the small plus button next to the Templates folder (on the Mac, click the disclosure triangle next to Templates).

   The templates defined for your Web site appear.

4. Select a template to display it in the Preview pane (**Figure 8.1**).

5. Click in the "Page title" field, and enter a title for your new Web page.

6. Click OK.

   Contribute creates the new page based on the template and marks an editable region in the draft page with a tab and a green outline (**Figure 8.2**).

✔ Tip

- Don't forget to link your new page to the rest of your site. See Chapter 6, "Working with Links," for more information about linking.

NEW PAGES FROM DREAMWEAVER TEMPLATES

Dreamweaver Template Details

This section is meant for the Dreamweaver designer who will be creating templates for Contribute users, but Contribute users might also want to understand the details and constraints in creating templates.

Dreamweaver templates are available to Contribute users who have access to the site and who have permission to access particular templates. *Permission groups,* set by the Contribute site administrator, give one or more Contribute users access to specified templates. For example, the administrator could give users in a human resources department access to only that department's templates. See Chapter 10 for more information about site administration in Contribute, or Chapter 11 for more about administering Contribute sites from Dreamweaver MX.

Dreamweaver users can save any HTML page as a template. Dreamweaver saves templates with the filename extension .dwt, in a folder called Templates in the root folder of the site—attributes that Contribute recognizes. If the Templates folder doesn't already exist on the server, Dreamweaver automatically creates it. Templates must be placed in the Templates folder to be correctly used by Contribute, so don't move templates to other folders. In fact, all kinds of problems can occur with templates if you change things (mainly they won't work correctly), so don't move the template files, don't move the Templates folder, and don't rename template files.

Automatic Updates

When a Dreamweaver template changes, Dreamweaver automatically updates all the pages based on that template. So you could, in principle, work on a page, and then come back later to work on it again and find that the page looks entirely different because the page designer has modified the template.

The advantage of templates is that designers don't have to go through dozens or hundreds of pages to update the look of a site; all they need to do is change the templates. Templates are also useful for updating page elements that aren't, strictly speaking, design-related. For example, the designer can update the copyright date on an entire site by simply changing the template file and then allowing Dreamweaver to ripple the changes through all the pages based on that template.

One thing to note is that a change to a template will only propagate to pages based on the template if the change is made in a locked region. Any changes made to an editable region will not be changed when the template is saved or updated.

When creating your templates in Dreamweaver, be sure to keep the target Contribute user in mind. This user is more familiar with Microsoft Word than with powerful (and complex) Web tools like Dreamweaver, so you should design the templates so that they are easily understood by nontechnical contributors and therefore make it easier to add content to the site. Consider doing one or more of the following:

◆ Clearly label the editable regions with names that describe what content they should contain. "Story text" is a better label than "Edit Region 1."

◆ If you are setting up templates for use on an intranet or in a collaborative environment, such as a team Web site for a group of people working on a project, it is usually best to keep your template design very simple and give your users one or more large, blank editable regions to work with. You don't need to worry too much about the look of such templates, since they will be for internal company use; keeping them flexible and usable is more important. Too many design restrictions will restrict the team members' ability to adapt the templates to their needs.

◆ Use text fonts consistently in your templates. It's preferable to apply font styles using Cascading Style Sheets (CSS).

◆ If you give the contributor the ability to style text, use Cascading Style Sheets to define your text styles.

◆ Use descriptive names for the CSS text styles so that users will know what they are for. Body text is a good name; modArial3 is not, even if you know exactly what it is.

continues on next page

- Unless it is necessary for users to style text, use the Contribute permission groups to disable this capability. If you deselect the "Allow users to apply styles" and "Allow users to apply fonts and sizes" options in the Styles and Fonts section of the Permission Group dialog, the user will not have access to the Style, Font, or Font Size menus in the toolbar. See the "Styles and Fonts permissions" section in Chapter 10 for more details.

- If you allow users to add images to templates, make sure they send the pages to you for review before they publish the page. Many Contribute users will not have the expertise or the software tools necessary to correctly prepare images for the Web—for example, properly resizing or compressing them. You could have a situation where users upload dozens of multi-megabyte files that came right off their digital cameras. See the "Letting Coworkers Review Your Pages" section in Chapter 3 for more information on page review.

- Create a set of instructions for the Contribute user that explain how to use your template, and then send the instructions via email. You'll save yourself time in the long run, because you won't have as many user mistakes to fix.

- Your site will be more useful if you create and include a separate style sheet designed for easy printing. Include a button in the locked portion of the template that the site visitor can use to access the print version of the page.

They Can't Touch the Code

Macromedia Contribute users not only can't view HTML source code from within the program, but they are also restricted by default from deleting or altering script tags; server-side includes; code tags such as ColdFusion, JSP, ASP, ASP.NET, and PHP tags; and form elements.

If you need to give some users the ability to modify this sort of code, you can do so on pages that don't use templates by deselecting the "Protect scripts and forms" option in the Editing section of the Permission Group dialog. It's a good idea to create a separate permissions group for these privileged users. If the page uses templates, however, you can't allow any code access.

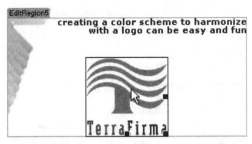

Figure 8.3 Contribute delineates the editable regions by a green outline and a tab with the region name.

Working with Editable Areas

Pages based on Dreamweaver templates show the editable regions in the draft window as areas outlined in green, with a tab and the editable region name (**Figure 8.3**). Editable regions are most often containers for text, but they can also contain images, tables, and other objects, such as Flash movies. Editable regions do not have to be devoted to only one type of content; text and images can share a region.

When the site designer uses Cascading Style Sheet (CSS) styles, he or she can assign styles to each region, which will be used for any content you add. When the site designer does not use CSS styles, you can use HTML styles (if the site administrator has granted you text-formatting privileges).

To work in an editable area:

1. Create a new page based on a Dreamweaver template, or open a draft page created from a Dreamweaver template.

2. Click within the editable region, and add your content.

✔ Tips

- The Dreamweaver-template creator can make Contribute users' work easier by giving meaningful names to the editable regions. For example, different editable regions on a page might be named Headline, Byline, and Body Text.

- Template creators can really help Contribute users by giving them a printout of a mockup page with the editable regions labeled and annotated with a description of each region.

Repeating regions

A *repeating region* is a section of a template that the user can duplicate as often as needed in a template-based page. Repeating regions are most often used by designers to allow users to create as many rows of a table as needed, without the designer's having to specify the table size in advance. The designer needs to create only the first row of the table, and then the user can duplicate that row as he or she adds content. The repeating region contains controls to add a region, subtract a region, move a region down, or move a region up (**Figure 8.4**).

Repeating regions in Dreamweaver must themselves contain editable regions as containers for content. Technically, a repeating region doesn't have to contain an editable region. However, if it doesn't, the user cannot add content.

To work in a repeating region:

1. Create or open a page based on a template that contains a repeating region.

2. Click within the editable regions in the repeating region, and make your edits.

3. Click the plus button to create another repeating region (**Figure 8.5**).

4. Make your edits within the new region.

5. (Optional) To rearrange regions, click in a region, and use the up and down arrows at the top of the repeating region to move it.

   or

   To remove a repeating region, click the minus button.

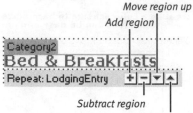

Figure 8.4 You can easily create and manipulate repeating regions with these controls.

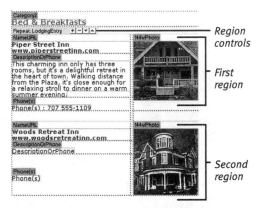

Figure 8.5 Clicking the plus button created the second instance of the repeating region (bottom). The second instance first appeared with the same picture as the one in the top region, which is the placeholder image from the template. I then replaced the images.

Figure 8.6 The info bar lets you know when you have editable template properties.

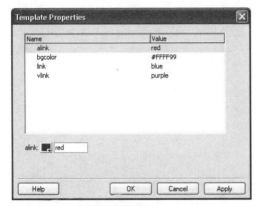

Figure 8.7 You can edit the template properties in the Template Properties dialog. When you select an available property, details about it appear below the list, allowing you to modify the property.

Setting Template Properties

Designers can create *optional regions* in templates that users can show or hide, depending on whether they are needed. Designers also have the option of letting users set the page background color or other properties of the page that may be page specific, such as the page title or keywords. Template properties are created by the template designer. Users can change properties with the Template Properties dialog.

To set template properties:

1. Begin editing a draft of the template-based page you want to change.

   The info bar lets you know that the template has editable template properties (**Figure 8.6**).

2. Choose Format > Template Properties.

   The Template Properties dialog appears (**Figure 8.7**).

3. Select a property in the Name list.

   Information about the property appears below the Name list.

4. Edit the property as needed.

   Depending on the property, different information appears below the Name list. When the property is a color, Contribute displays a color box that, when clicked, brings up the color picker.

5. Click OK.

WORKING WITH EXTERNAL DOCUMENTS

9

Macromedia Contribute gives you the ability to edit Web sites, and in previous chapters we've seen how you can use Contribute to create and work with HTML files, image files, and even some media files, such as Macromedia Flash files. In Chapter 6, "Working with Links," we touched on Contribute's ability to link to other file types.

A new feature in Contribute 2 for Windows, FlashPaper, turns any document you can print into a Flash file that is inserted into your draft page. This Flash document can be read in almost all browsers, using the widely-installed Flash Player.

continues on next page

Contribute has special capabilities for working with documents from two other applications, Microsoft Word and Microsoft Excel. Contribute can create links to these documents; this merely uploads the files to your Web site, but on the Windows version of Contribute, you can import the contents of the documents directly into Contribute, turning that content into Web pages that you can then manage and edit within Contribute. In order to import Word or Excel documents into Contribute, you'll need to have these programs installed on your Windows machine. If you don't, you can still make links to the documents, but you won't be able to import or edit them.

On Macintosh, you can copy and paste from Word and Excel, and Contribute knows how to do "Smart Copy and Paste" so that the copied information appears in your Contribute draft page formatted correctly.

Using External Documents

First, let's define our terms. For the purpose of this chapter, I'm calling a document that isn't created in Contribute, and isn't an HTML page, an *external document*. That's because when you attempt to edit these documents in Contribute, the program hands off the editing job to another application and refers to this task as Editing Documents in External Applications. You've already seen some of this external editing with image files in Chapter 5, "Working with Images," when Contribute called upon Macromedia Fireworks as an external image editor to modify a graphic.

Contribute for Windows can directly import the contents of a Word or Excel document and turn it into an HTML page. Contribute for Macintosh can copy and paste the contents of an open Word or Excel document into a draft page. On both platforms, Contribute can upload a copy of the document to your Web site and create a link to it. See the "Linking to Local Files" section in Chapter 6 for more information about linking and uploading files. When visitors select the link, their Web browser downloads the file, which then needs to be opened in Word or Excel.

Contribute for Windows' import capability for Word and Excel documents offers a great way to make this content part of your Web site without requiring your site's visitors to own the Microsoft Office programs. You can drag and drop a Word or Excel document from the Windows desktop into Contribute, which will read this *source document*, convert it into HTML, and display it in Contribute's editing mode. You can then make any changes and publish the page to your Web site as usual.

continues on next page

Contribute for Macintosh doesn't have capabilities as complete for importing Office documents. Instead of being able to convert Microsoft Office documents in Contribute, or drag them in from the Finder, you must copy content from Word or Excel and paste it into Contribute. When you paste into Contribute, the program parses the information and performs what Macromedia calls a "Smart Copy and Paste" which maintains the formatting that was in the Office document. This doesn't always work perfectly, but it often works quite well.

When you bring an Office document into Contribute, you are making a copy of the original document. Any changes you make within Contribute will *not* be reflected in the original Word or Excel document on your computer. Similarly, changes you make in Word or Excel to the original source document will not be reflected on your Web site. If you modify a source document and want to update your Web site, you need to delete the Web page with the now-superceded content, reimport the document into Contribute, and publish the new page.

Besides Word and Excel documents, Contribute is compatible with external documents in pretty much any format, such as Adobe Acrobat files, Microsoft PowerPoint presentations, QuickTime movies, MP3 music files, and Windows Media movie files. When you add one of these files to your Web site, Contribute uploads the file to the site and adds a link to the file. When a site visitor clicks the link, the file downloads to his or her computer.

✔ Tips

- Contribute uploads files other than HTML documents to a folder on your Web site called documents. Contribute will create this folder if necessary, and will place it in the same directory as the page that contains the link to the external document.

- While it is easy to upload most file types to your website, it is up to the abilities of the users' browser to play or display these file types. Files such as mp3s or movies may require browser plugins.

Cleaner Office Documents

Recent versions of Microsoft Office, such as Office 2000 and Office XP on Windows, and Office v. X for Macintosh, have the built-in ability to save Word and Excel documents as Web pages. You might be tempted to save a document from one of these applications as a Web page and then upload the page to your Web site. But when you use Contribute, you should resist the temptation, because Office documents imported into Contribute and then turned into Web pages end up being smaller in size (and therefore quicker to load), and compliant with accepted Web standards.

The problem is that when the Office applications save a document as a Web page, the HTML code created includes lots of excess or Microsoft-specific code that is designed to enable these Web pages to be brought back into Word or Excel more easily, but that most browsers don't need. This isn't a small amount of extra code, either; in test pages saved as Web pages from Word versus imported into Contribute, Word's resulting HTML files were as much as three times the size of Contribute's files.

Contribute's HTML-creation engine is based on Macromedia Dreamweaver's engine, and therefore Contribute inherits Dreamweaver's excellent ability to write clean, standards-compliant code. Standards compliance is important because compliant pages display well in any modern browser, whether that browser is running on a Windows machine, a Macintosh, or even a PDA or cell phone. Standards-based Web sites are also better for people with disabilities, especially the vision impaired who use audio screen readers or greatly enlarged text. Depending on where you're working, standards compliance may even be the law; many government agencies are now required to make their site accessible for people with disabilities. For more information about legal requirements for accessibility, see Section508.com (www.section508.com), named for the section of the 1998 Rehabilitation Act that established the federal accessibility requirements.

For more information about Web standards, visit www.webstandards.org, the Web site of the Web Standards Project, a volunteer organization that works to promote standards.

CLEANER OFFICE DOCUMENTS

Importing Word or Excel Documents

There are two ways to insert a Word or Excel document into Contribute for Windows. The easiest method is to drag and drop the file from the Windows desktop into Contribute's editing window. Alternatively, you can use commands in Contribute's Insert menu. On Macintosh, you'll copy and paste from the Office application into Contribute.

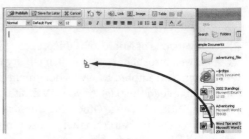

Figure 9.1 Drag a Word or Excel file from the Windows desktop into Contribute's editing window to import the file.

To import a Word or Excel document into Contribute (Windows):

1. Choose File > New Page, or press Ctrl-N.

   or

   Browse to an existing page on your Web site, click the Edit Page button, and then place the insertion point where you want to add the imported content.

2. Drag the file from the Windows desktop into Contribute's editing window (**Figure 9.1**).

   or

   Choose Insert > Microsoft Word Document (or Insert > Microsoft Excel Document).

3. If you use one of the Insert commands, Contribute displays an Open dialog. Navigate to the document you want, select it, and click Open.

   The document's contents appear in the current draft.

   or

   If you dragged the document into Contribute, the Insert Microsoft Word or Excel Document dialog appears (**Figure 9.2**).

Figure 9.2 The choice is yours: Add a link to the document file, convert the document to FlashPaper, or add the document's content to the existing page.

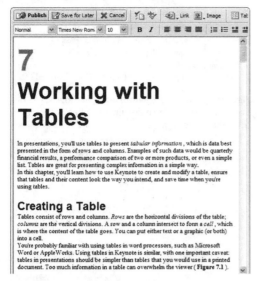

Figure 9.3 The Word document is converted, and its content appears in the editing window. Note how Contribute can maintain much of the document's formatting.

4. You have three choices:

▲ You can insert the document's contents into the current page.

▲ You can insert the document as FlashPaper.

▲ You can choose to create a link to the document.

Make your choice, then click OK.

Either the link or the document's content appears in the current draft (**Figure 9.3**). The FlashPaper option will be covered in the "Inserting External Documents as FlashPaper" section later in this chapter.

5. (Optional) Edit the document to suit the needs of your Web page.

Some formatting of the original may be lost in the conversion.

6. Click Publish.

✔ Tips

- You can set a user preference to have Contribute always either add the contents of the Word or Excel document, turn the document into FlashPaper, or insert a link to the document. Choose Edit > Preferences, then select the General category. In the "Microsoft Office documents" section, select one of the four choices (**Figure 9.4**).

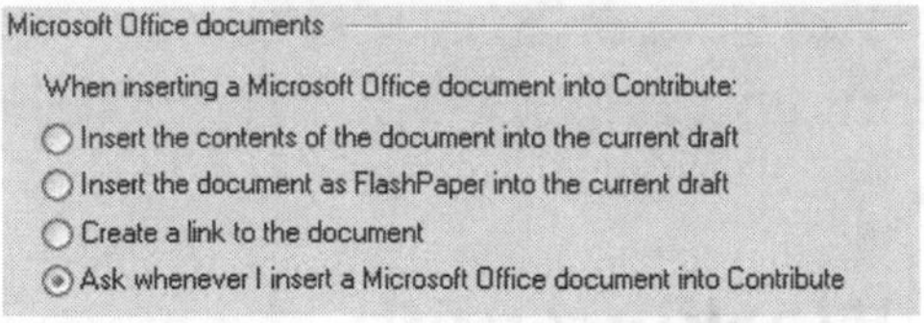

Figure 9.4 You can set a preference for how Contribute treats Office documents when you drag them into the program.

- If the Insert > Microsoft Word Document or Insert > Microsoft Excel Document menu items are unavailable, it is probably because you don't have one or both of those programs installed. You can still get the content of the document into a Contribute draft page by having a coworker with the programs save the document as a text file, which you can then open with Notepad and paste into Contribute.

- If you have inserted a link to a Word or Excel document, and your site's visitor has Word or Excel on his or her machine, clicking the link downloads the file and opens the application.

- If an Office document is too large to import, you can work around Contribute's limitation by using Word or Excel to split the document into multiple smaller documents, and then import each document into its own new Contribute pages using Insert > Microsoft Word Document or Insert > Microsoft Excel Document. Then you can create links between the new pages.

- If the document you dragged into Contribute is too large (greater than 300K when converted to HTML), Contribute displays a dialog that suggests you insert the file into your page as a link.

- If you need to import a file that will be more than 150K of HTML, Contribute displays a warning that the import may take a while to process. The import will still work properly, but the program might appear to have stalled. Be patient; the page will appear when Contribute finishes the import. If the import is too big, Contribute lets you know with the dialog that suggests you add the Office document as a link.

- Microsoft Office 97 does not have the ability to add the contents of a Word or Excel document by dragging and dropping it into Contribute. Instead, dragging and dropping always adds a link to the document. A partial workaround is to open Word 97 or Excel 97, copy the document's content to the Clipboard, and paste it into Contribute's editing window. Unfortunately, the pasted text will lose its text formatting.

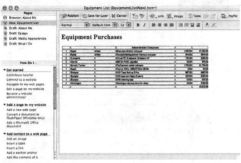

Figure 9.5 The copied portion of this Excel worksheet (top) appears with formatting intact when it is pasted into Contribute (bottom).

To import a Word or Excel document into Contribute (Macintosh):

1. Use Word or Excel to open the document you want to bring into Contribute.

2. Select the part of the document you want to copy into Contribute.

   or

   Press Cmd-A to select the entire document.

3. Choose Edit > Copy, or press Cmd-C.

4. Switch to Contribute.

5. Choose File > New Page, or press Ctrl-N.

   or

   Browse to an existing page on your Web site, click the Edit Page button, and then place the insertion point where you want to add the imported content.

6. Choose Edit > Paste, or press Cmd-V.

   After a short delay while Contribute parses the contents of the Clipboard, the content appears in Contribute (**Figure 9.5**).

✔ Tips

- Documents pasted from Excel will be converted into tables in Contribute, but you will probably want to increase the size of the table text in Contribute.

- Documents that contain graphics will not bring the images along with the text. A placeholder for the image will appear in the Contribute document with a "broken link" icon. In fact, you can't copy and paste graphics from any other application into Contribute.

Office Document Import Limitations

Contribute does a good job of importing many types of Office documents, but it has some limitations you should know about. The main limitation is that if the HTML file created from the Word or Excel document will be greater than 300K, Contribute inserts a link to the document rather than importing the document's content.

Word limitations. Besides the document size limit mentioned above, Contribute also has difficulty importing Word documents that have complex page layouts. For example, multiple-page Word documents that make use of text boxes for layout (**Figure 9.6**) often import as a single large image, usually missing the contents of the text boxes. Worse, the image does not look like the original page, and could have incorrect layout or even distorted type and images (**Figure 9.7**). You're better off importing such documents as FlashPaper (if you're using the Windows version of Contribute), or creating complex layouts in Dreamweaver, saving them as templates, and inserting just the text and images in Contribute.

continues on next page

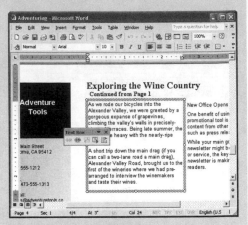

Figure 9.6 This desktop-publishing style Word document uses text boxes for layout control.

Figure 9.7 Importing complex layouts from Word into Contribute doesn't always give the best results. This file imported as a distorted image.

Figure 9.8 Excel files convert into complex HTML tables.

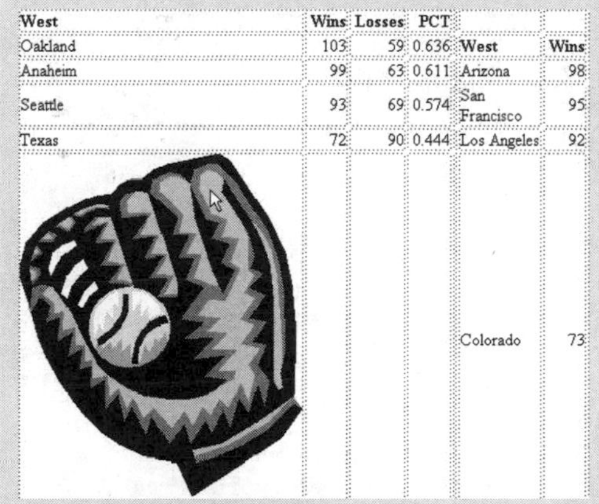

Figure 9.9 Pictures in the Excel file might mean distorted tables in Contribute.

A good rule of thumb is that if the document requires that you view it in Word's Print Layout View in order to see the page's elements, the document won't import well into Contribute (even Word itself doesn't do a good job of saving these kinds of documents as Web pages). This isn't a hard-and-fast rule, however, so it's usually worth at least attempting to import a Word document into Contribute that you think might be problematic. You might get lucky.

Excel limitations. When importing Excel worksheets into Contribute, the worksheet comes into Contribute as a complex table, with the worksheet's cells converted to cells in the HTML table (**Figure 9.8**). You can work with the imported table as you would any other table in Contribute (see Chapter 7, "Creating Tables"). If the Excel document contains an image (such as clip art), the image is placed into one cell in the HTML table, and the rest of the table cells resize to accommodate the picture (**Figure 9.9**), giving you perhaps unintended results.

Inserting External Documents as FlashPaper
(Windows-only)

One of the new features in Contribute 2 is the ability to convert any document that can be printed into a Macromedia Flash movie, and to place that movie into a Contribute draft page. That Flash movie can be displayed by any Web browser that has the free Flash Player 6; Macromedia claims that more than 98% of Internet users have the Flash Player.

FlashPaper documents are converted into the Flash file format using a printer driver called the FlashPaper Printer that is installed when you install Contribute 2 for Windows. The FlashPaper Printer places the content of the document inside a simple document viewer interface, then hands the completed FlashPaper document back to Contribute, which inserts it into the web page. The FlashPaper document can then be aligned and resized within the Contribute draft page as you would any other graphic image. Since it is Flash, it can be resized without a loss of quality.

Because the Flash file format is especially efficient, a FlashPaper document is usually smaller, often dramatically so, than the source document. For example, in tests that I ran, the FlashPaper version of an 8 Mb Adobe Acrobat (PDF) document was only 2.6 Mb in size. A 584 Kb Word document ended up as a 182 Kb FlashPaper file. There is a big benefit to smaller download sizes for documents, as it means that more users will be likely to wait while the document downloads.

While you can use FlashPaper in place of a PDF file in many applications, FlashPaper is not a replacement for PDF files. FlashPaper turns the document into a graphic, so you can't select text or search a FlashPaper document. PDF also has many collaboration and security features that FlashPaper lacks, such as annotation, digital signatures, and encryption.

Another important limitation is that you cannot edit a FlashPaper document. If you need to update the document, you must make changes to the document you originally converted, then convert it again to a FlashPaper document.

Unfortunately, creating FlashPaper is a Windows-only technology, at least for Contribute 2, though you can view FlashPaper documents with any browser on any platform that supports the Flash Player. Macromedia has stated that it hopes to bring FlashPaper creation to the Macintosh version of Contribute in the future. Even on Windows, FlashPaper isn't fully supported in Contribute 2; it is only supported on Windows 2000 and XP, so Windows 98 and Me users are out of luck.

You can create a FlashPaper document in one of two ways:

- ◆ Convert and insert a document in Contribute. The entire external document will be converted into FlashPaper and inserted into your draft page.

- ◆ Convert a document in another application, then add the FlashPaper document to a Contribute draft page. The good thing about this approach is that you can select a section or pages of the document to convert to FlashPaper.

INSERTING EXTERNAL DOCUMENTS AS FLASHPAPER

To insert a document as FlashPaper:

1. Browse to an existing page on your web site, click the Edit Page button, and then place the insertion point where you want to add the FlashPaper document.

2. Choose Insert > Document as FlashPaper. An Open dialog appears.

3. Navigate to and select the document that you want to convert, then click Open. The FlashPaper Options dialog appears (**Figure 9.10**).

4. Choose the page orientation for the FlashPaper page.

   Your choices are Portrait or Landscape orientation.

5. Choose a page size from the pop-up menu. The standard available page sizes are Letter, Tabloid, Letter, Legal, Executive, A3, A4, A5, B4, and B5.

6. (Optional) If you want to set a custom size for the FlashPaper document, click the Custom button, then type the height and width dimensions you want. You can also choose inches or millimeters as units from the pop-up menu.

7. Click OK.

   Contribute converts the document to FlashPaper and inserts it in the page (**Figure 9.11**).

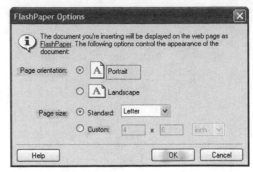

Figure 9.10 The FlashPaper Options dialog allows you to set the page orientation and page size.

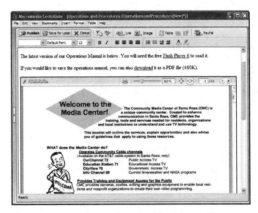

Figure 9.11 After conversion, the FlashPaper document appears in your draft page. I've closed the Sidebar in this figure to show the FlashPaper document better.

✔ Tips

- Contribute site administrators can set an option to ensure accessibility of your web pages by disabled users, and turning this setting on disables insertion of Flash content, including FlashPaper.

- If you want to post content on the Web that you don't want people to copy and paste into their own documents, FlashPaper is a good way to protect your content, since text in FlashPaper cannot be selected.

The FlashPaper Toolbar

FlashPaper comes with its own user interface that appears at the top of the FlashPaper document. This interface allows you to zoom in (or out) on the document, and navigate through the document (**Figure 9.12**).

- ◆ To print, click the **Printer icon**. Note that this will print just the FlashPaper document, not the entire page in which it is embedded.

- ◆ Use the **Zoom slider** to change the document magnification from 25% up to 250%. You can also type a number in the **Zoom text box**.

- ◆ To see the entire page in the FlashPaper viewer, click the **Fit in Viewer button**.

- ◆ If you want the width of the page to fill the viewer, click the **Fit Width button**.

- ◆ To jump to a page in your document, type a number in the **Select page** field.

- ◆ You can page through the document by using the scroll bar, or by clicking the **Page Forward** or **Page Back** buttons.

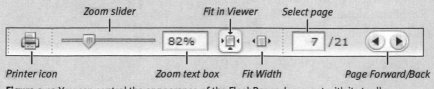

Zoom slider   Fit in Viewer   Select page

Printer icon   Zoom text box   Fit Width   Page Forward/Back

Figure 9.12 You can control the appearance of the FlashPaper document with its toolbar.

To convert a document to FlashPaper in another application:

1. In an application that created or views the document that you want to convert to FlashPaper, choose File > Print.

   The Print dialog appears.

2. In the list of available printers, choose FlashPaper Printer (**Figure 9.13**).

3. (Optional) Set the printer options you want to apply to the converted document.

   This allows you to set a page range to convert to FlashPaper.

4. (Optional) You can click the Properties button to bring up and adjust the FlashPaper Options dialog.

5. Click OK.

   The document is converted to FlashPaper and appears in the stand-alone FlashPaper viewer.

6. Choose File > Save to save the FlashPaper document to your hard drive.

7. Navigate to where you want to save the FlashPaper document, then click OK.

8. Switch to Contribute.

9. Browse to a page on your web site, click the Edit Page button, and then place the insertion point where you want to add the FlashPaper document.

10. Drag the FlashPaper document from the Windows desktop into your draft page.

    or

    Choose Insert > Flash Movie > From My Computer, then navigate to and open the FlashPaper document.

    The FlashPaper document appears in your draft page.

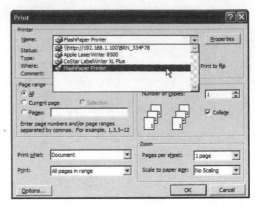

Figure 9.13 Choose the FlashPaper Printer in the Print dialog (this example is from Microsoft Word).

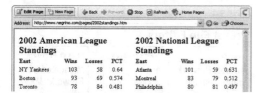

2002 American League Standings				2002 National League Standings			
East	Wins	Losses	PCT	East	Wins	Losses	PCT
NY Yankees	103	58	0.64	Atlanta	101	59	0.631
Boston	93	69	0.574	Montreal	83	79	0.512
Toronto	78	84	0.481	Philadelphia	80	81	0.497

Figure 9.14 Begin editing an imported Word or Excel document by clicking the Edit Page button.

Editing Imported Office Documents

Because an imported Word or Excel document has been converted into an HTML document in the process of importing it into Contribute, you edit it as you would any other Web page in Contribute.

Don't forget that the HTML document you are editing is a copy of the original source document, and changes you make in it will not be reflected in the original.

To edit an imported Word or Excel document:

1. Browse to the page you want to edit.

2. Click Edit Page in the toolbar, or choose File > Edit Page, or press Ctrl-Shift-E (Cmd-Shift-E) (**Figure 9.14**).

   The page appears in Contribute's editing window, and the page draft's name appears in the Pages panel of the sidebar.

3. Make the changes you want.

4. Click Publish to save your changes to the Web site.

Editing Other Document Types

To modify any content on your Web site other than an HTML file, you need to edit that content in the application in which it was created. For example, if you have an image file on your site, you need to use an image editing application to modify it. But you have to use Contribute to begin the editing process so that Contribute keeps proper track of the edited copy of the file on your site. By using Contribute to manage the editing process, you can take advantage of Contribute's special features, such as rollbacks, which let you revert to a previous version of any published page or document. See Chapter 3, "Building Web Pages," for more information on rollbacks.

In order to edit a document, such as an image, in an external application, Contribute must know which application you want to use to edit a given file type. Contribute comes with a list of preset file types, as shown in **Table 9.1**, but you can add additional editing applications for each file type. You'll need to designate one application as the primary editing application for that file type.

For example, you might want to change Contribute's default file editor for image files, such as JPEG files. Contribute's default file editor for JPEG files is Fireworks. If you don't own Fireworks, you can add a different editor, such as Adobe Photoshop or cheaper alternatives such as Windows Paint or GraphicConverter for the Mac as the file editor of choice.

Table 9.1

Preset File Editors		
FILE TYPE	FILE EXTENSION	PRESET EDITOR
Portable Network Graphics image	.png	Macromedia Fireworks MX
GIF image	.gif	Macromedia Fireworks MX
JPEG image	.jpg, .jpe, .jpeg	Macromedia Fireworks MX
Bitmap image	.bmp	Macromedia Fireworks MX
Text file	.txt	Notepad (TextEdit on Mac)
XML file	.xml	Notepad (TextEdit on Mac)
Word file	.doc	Microsoft Word
Excel file	.xls	Microsoft Excel
PowerPoint file	.ppt	Microsoft PowerPoint

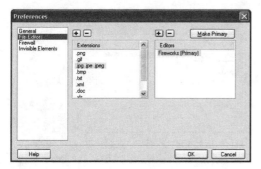

Figure 9.15 You can add file editors for any given file type.

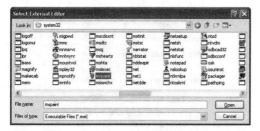

Figure 9.16 Navigate to the editing application you want to use.

To add a file editor:

1. Choose Edit > Preferences (Contribute > Preferences).

   The Preferences dialog appears.

2. Select the File Editors category (**Figure 9.15**).

3. From the Extensions list, select the file extension for which you want to add a file editor.

4. Click the plus button above the Editors list.

   The Select External Editor dialog appears (**Figure 9.16**).

5. Navigate to the program you want to use as a file editor, select it, and click Open.

   The new editor appears in the Editors list.

6. (Optional) Select the new editor and click Make Primary.

7. Click OK to save your preferences.

✔ Tip

■ If you have Dreamweaver MX installed, change the file editor for XML files from the default, which is Notepad on Windows and TextEdit on Mac, to Dreamweaver. The latter program's Code View has much better capabilities for editing XML files.

To edit an external document:

1. In Contribute's Browse mode, click the link to the external document you want to edit, or click Choose in the toolbar.

   The Choose File on Website dialog appears (**Figure 9.17**).

2. Navigate to the file you want to edit, select the file, and click OK.

   Depending on the type of file you are browsing, the File Download dialog may appear (**Figure 9.18**). If it does, click Open.

   If the file can be displayed by Contribute's browser, it will appear. Otherwise, the File Placeholder screen will appear (**Figure 9.19**).

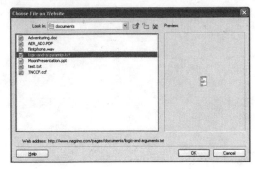

Figure 9.17 Select a file on your Web site for editing in an external application.

Figure 9.18 If necessary, the File Download dialog creates a temporary copy of the external file on your hard disk, so that it can be edited.

Figure 9.19 The File Placeholder screen tells you that Contribute can't display the type of file you've selected. Click Edit to launch the external file editor.

Figure 9.20 Contribute creates a draft page, tells you that it has handed the file off to an external editor, then switches to that editor.

Figure 9.21 Make your changes to the file in the external editor, then save and close it before returning to Contribute.

3. Click Edit in the toolbar.

Contribute creates a new draft page, displays the Editing Draft in Another Application screen (**Figure 9.20**), and launches the file editor listed in Contribute's preferences for the kind of file you're editing (**Figure 9.21**).

4. Edit the file in the external file editor. When you are finished, save and close the file, then return to Contribute.

5. Contribute will still be displaying the Editing Draft in Another Application screen. Click the Publish button to save the draft page to the server.

✔ Tip

- If the Edit button is not available in step 3, check Contribute's Preferences to see if you have set a file editor in the File Editors category for the kind of file you're editing.

EDITING OTHER DOCUMENT TYPES

SITE
ADMINISTRATION

10

Site administrators manage Contribute Web sites. The administrators do this mainly by controlling who has access to the site and by specifying the editing capabilities of the content creators using Contribute. Contribute users can be designated as site administrators, or sites can be administered using Macromedia Dreamweaver MX (version 6.1 or later).

As a site administrator, you are responsible for determining which users have editing access to your Web site, deciding the level of editing access (called *permissions*) of each user, and creating and distributing connection keys to your site's users. You typically define *permission groups* for your site and assign individual contributors to a group. The permissions you assign to a group determine the nature of the editing access that members of the group have on your site.

In this chapter you'll learn how permissions work, how to become a site administrator, and how to create and modify sets of permissions you can assign to groups of users.

SITE ADMINISTRATION

Becoming an Administrator

Contribute contains all the tools you need to become a site administrator, define and set permission groups, and send connection keys to site contributors. You can also administer Contribute Web sites using Dreamweaver MX 6.1 or later. See Chapter 11, "Managing Sites with Dreamweaver," for more information. Contribute stores permission settings on the server in the *shared settings file*, which all Contribute users of the site can read. When an administrator is assigned for a site, Contribute (or Dreamweaver) creates the shared settings file, as well as several other files and folders it uses to maintain its site management.

You can become the administrator of any Web site that doesn't already have an administrator. To see whether a Web site has a current administrator, choose Edit > My Connections (Contribute > My Connections), and look for the Web site in the list in the My Connections dialog (**Figure 10.1**). The list shows the email address of the administrator, if one exists, or shows <No administrator> if one does not.

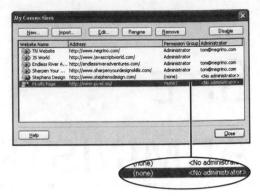

Figure 10.1 Sites without administrators show <No administrator> in the My Connections dialog.

Figure 10.2 Answer affirmatively when Contribute asks if you want to become the site administrator.

Figure 10.3 You need to type and confirm a new password to become a site administrator.

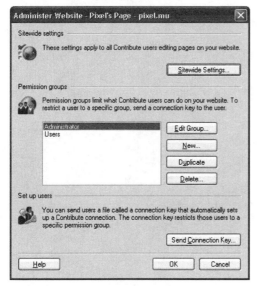

Figure 10.4 The Administer Website dialog allows you to apply settings for the entire site, add and maintain permission groups, and send connection keys.

To become a site administrator:

1. Choose Edit > Administer Websites (Contribute > Administer Websites), then choose the site you want to administer from the cascading menu.

   Contribute checks the site, and if the site does not have an administrator, it asks if you want to become the administrator (**Figure 10.2**).

   (If the site already has an administrator, Contribute prompts you for the administrator password. Because you want to become the site administrator, you've made a mistake and should click Cancel in the password dialog.)

2. Click Yes.

   The Administrator Password dialog appears (**Figure 10.3**). Because you are adding administration to the Web site, Contribute has the "Old password" field disabled.

3. Type a password in the "New password" field, and then enter it again in the "Confirm new password" field.

   If your two entries don't match, Contribute alerts you and allows you to retype the confirmation password.

4. Click OK.

   The Administer Website dialog appears (**Figure 10.4**).

5. Make changes to sitewide settings or permission groups, as detailed later in this chapter.

   You can also send connection keys to users from this dialog.

6. Click OK to save your administrative changes.

✔ **Tips**

- You must have already created a connection to a site before you can become its administrator.

- If Contribute has the Administer Websites menu disabled, you might be working offline. Check to see if the File > Work Offline (Contribute > Work Offline) menu choice is active; if it is, select it to toggle Contribute back to online status. Of course, you need an active Internet connection to work online.

- You can send connection keys to coworkers via email from the Administer Website dialog. See "Sharing Site Connections" in Chapter 2 for details.

- You can use a Web-based mail program, such as Hotmail or Yahoo! Mail, to send connection keys, but doing so isn't recommended. If you want to use a Web-based mail program, save the connection key on your computer and manually attach the file to the outgoing email message.

- Contribute connection keys are XML files that are encrypted using 128-bit encryption, the same level of encryption used by Web browsers for e-commerce and online banking. It's possible to compromise this type of encryption, but doing so takes a lot of time and computing resources, making it impractical. For most purposes, connection keys you send via email are secure. Just make sure you transmit the user's password separately from the connection key: A different email, fax, or phone call all work well.

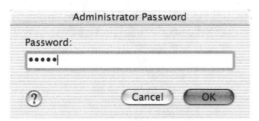

Figure 10.5 Type the administrator password to gain access to the Administer Website dialog.

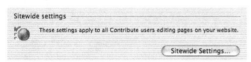

Figure 10.6 The "Sitewide settings" section of the Administer Website dialog.

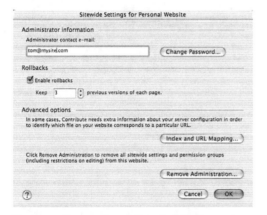

Figure 10.7 You can change the administrator password in the Sitewide Settings dialog.

Figure 10.8 To change the administrator password, you need to type the old password and then type the new password twice.

Assigning Sitewide Settings

Sitewide settings are administrative settings that affect the general administration of a Web site and all the Contribute users who connect to it.

Changing administrator email and password

If you are the administrator of a Web site and you want to pass the responsibility on to someone else, you'll need to change the administrator's email contact address and the administrator password for the site.

To change the administrator contact or password:

1. Choose Edit > Administer Websites (Contribute > Administer Websites), and then choose the Web site you want to change from the cascading menu.

   The Administrator Password dialog appears (**Figure 10.5**).

2. Type the administrator password, and then click OK.

   The Administer Website dialog appears with the Sitewide settings button (**Figure 10.6**).

3. Click Sitewide Settings.

   The Sitewide Settings dialog appears (**Figure 10.7**).

4. Type the email address for the new administrator.

   or

   Click Change Password. In the Change Administrator Password dialog (**Figure 10.8**), type the old password and the new password, and then type the new password again to confirm. Click OK to return to the Sitewide Settings dialog.

5. Click OK to save your administrative changes.

✔ Tips

- If you can't choose a Web site from the Administer Websites cascading menu, Contribute may have disabled that site. Choose Edit > My Connections (Contribute > My Connections), and then look at the Web site entry in the My Connections dialog. If the Web site icon has a red slash through it, select the Website connection and click the Enable button.

- If you forget the administrator password, you can't get it back. You can, however, eliminate the password from the site by deleting it from the shared settings file, using Dreamweaver or any text-editing program (you can't use Contribute to delete the password). Deleting the password from the shared settings file resets the site password to *blank*—that is, the site has no password. To delete the password, open the root folder of your Contribute Web site and find the folder named _mm (for security reasons, you should use the server file system to allow the Contribute users read-only access to the _mm folder, but you, the administrator, must have read and write privileges). Inside the _mm folder you'll find a file named contribute.xml, which is the shared settings file. Open the file in Dreamweaver or a text editor, and look for <admin_password value='xxxxxxxx' /> in the file. Delete the encoded string listed between the single quotes, signified by the xxxxxxxx. Then save the shared settings file back to the Web server. After you save the file, you can once again administer your Contribute Web site. Go to Edit > Administer Websites (Contribute > Administer Websites) as you would normally, only this time do not type a password in the Administrator Password dialog before clicking OK. You should be sure to re-create an administrator password as described in this section.

- Changing the administrator password periodically can help protect the security of your site.

Figure 10.9 The Rollbacks section of the Sitewide Settings dialog allows you to set up to 99 rollback versions (but you probably don't want that many).

Enabling Rollbacks

Contribute can maintain up to 99 previous versions of each Web page on your site. For more information about how you can use rollbacks to revert to previous versions of your Web pages, see "Rolling Back to Previous Page Versions" in Chapter 3. Pg. 63

By default, Contribute saves three rollback versions of each page. Before you increase this number, you need to consider the effects of an increase on the amount of disk space your site will take up on your Web server, because Contribute saves the rollback versions of the pages, plus any associated files such as images, on the server in a special folder named _baks. Each version of the page takes up the same amount of space. You can see that if you have dozens or even hundreds of pages on a site, and each page has at least three versions (and more if you increase the number of allowable rollback versions), you can quickly use up a significant amount of server disk space.

To enable or change the number of rollbacks:

1. Choose Edit > Administer Websites (Contribute > Administer Websites), and then choose the Web site you want to change from the cascading menu.
   The Administrator Password dialog appears.

2. Type the administrator password, and then click OK.
   The Administer Website dialog appears.

3. Click Sitewide Settings.
   The Sitewide Settings dialog appears.

4. In the Rollbacks section (**Figure 10.9**), select the "Enable rollbacks" check box to make rollbacks active, or deselect it to turn rollbacks off.

continues on next page

5. If Contribute has rollbacks enabled, type a number in the "Keep previous versions of each page" field, or use the arrow buttons to set the number of rollbacks.

6. Click OK to return to the Administer Website dialog.

7. Click OK to save your administrative changes.

Index and URL mapping

When you start Contribute, it connects to your Web sites and looks for a number of items that help it determine the configuration of your Web server. One of the things Contribute needs to find is the *index page* for the site, the Web page displayed by default when a visitor browses to the site. For example, if you type the address http://www.peachpit.com/ into a browser, the page that is displayed may actually have the URL http://www.peachpit.com/index.html. Web servers are set to present the index page for a site when a visitor doesn't specify a page in the Web site. The Web server defaults to the index page rather than present the user with a page not found error message.

The most common default index-page filenames are

    index.html
    index.htm
    default.html
    default.htm

There are many other possible default index filenames, and Contribute comes with a list of 30 possible names. The program works through these names sequentially when browsing a Web server. If this list doesn't offer the names you want, you can add your own default index filenames, and you can also reorder the list if you want.

Contribute can also handle *alternate Web site addresses*. For example, the Web server may be set to send a visitor to the default

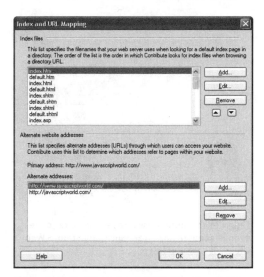

Figure 10.10 Use the Index and URL Mapping dialog to fine-tune the index pages and Web sites that Contribute looks for.

index page whether the visitor browses to either http://www.peachpit.com/ or http://peachpit.com/. Contribute maintains a list of alternate Web site addresses so that it knows the different addresses refer to the same site. The address doesn't have to be similar for Contribute to understand that it is the same site; for example, you can configure Contribute to recognize an entirely different domain, say http://www.reallygoodbooks.com/, as the same site as http://www.peachpit.com/.

To change index or URL mapping:

1. Choose Edit > Administer Websites (Contribute > Administer Websites), and then choose the Web site you want to change from the cascading menu.

   The Administrator Password dialog appears.

2. Type the administrator password, and then click OK.

   The Administer Website dialog appears.

3. Click Sitewide Settings.

   The Sitewide Settings dialog appears.

4. In the Advanced options section of the dialog, click Index and URL Mapping.

   The Index and URL Mapping dialog appears (**Figure 10.10**).

5. In the "Index files" section, use the Add, Edit, and Remove buttons or the up and down arrows to make changes to the "Index files" list.

   or

   In the "Alternate website addresses" section, use the Add, Edit, and Remove buttons to make changes.

6. Click OK to return to the Sitewide Settings dialog.

7. Click OK to return to the Administer Website dialog.

8. Click OK to save your administrative changes.

✔ Tip

■ Some Web sites use port numbers to choose between different versions of a site. For example, a Web site that has localizations for different languages may have the Web site for one language at www.mysite.com and the other at www.mysite.com:8080. Contribute considers a Web address that uses a different port number to be a different Web site. If you want Contribute to treat two Web addresses with different port numbers as the same site, you must add these Web addresses to the "Alternate addresses" field.

Removing administration

You can remove Contribute administration from the Web site. Removing administration deletes the sitewide settings file and therefore also deletes all the permission groups from the site.

To remove administration from a Web site:

1. Choose Edit > Administer Websites (Contribute > Administer Websites), and then choose the Web site you wish to change from the cascading menu.

   The Administrator Password dialog appears.

2. Type the administrator password, and then click OK.

   The Administer Website dialog appears.

3. Click Sitewide Settings.

   The Sitewide Settings dialog appears.

4. In the "Advanced options" section of the dialog, click Remove Administration.

5. Contribute displays two successive warning alerts asking if you're sure you want to remove administration for the site (**Figure 10.11**).

6. Click Yes to both warnings.

   The Administer Website dialog closes.

✔ Tips

- Removing administration does not remove the rollback files or the Design Notes (files that are accessible to Dreamweaver users). In order to delete these items from a site, you must use Dreamweaver or an FTP program.

- Removing administration is not the same as removing the connection. If you want to delete the connection, choose Edit > My Connections (Contribute > My Connections), select the connection in the My Connections dialog, and click Remove.

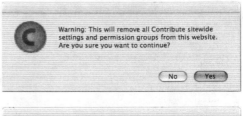

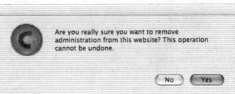

Figure 10.11 Contribute wants to make sure you're serious about removing administration from a Web site, so it asks you twice.

- Whether you want to remove administration or remove the connection, be sure to publish or cancel any draft pages from that Web site first.

Figure 10.12 You begin assigning permissions in the Administer Website dialog.

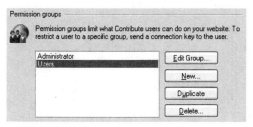

Figure 10.13 Select the group for which you want to assign or change permissions.

Assigning Permissions

Contribute users can't choose which permission group they belong to. Rather, the site administrator assigns users to permission groups. By default, Contribute supplies two permission groups for each Web site: Administrator and Users. Generally speaking, the Administrator group has more control over the Web site than the Users group. For example, the Administrator group, by default, has the permission to delete pages, and the Users group does not. You can redefine the default permissions of each group. In this section, we explore the permissions you can assign.

Contribute assigns many permissions by default, and in many cases you may find that these defaults work well. On the other hand, if you need specific control of your site, you can set permissions to be as loose or as restrictive as you like.

You can also create and change your own permission groups, of course. See the "Creating Permission Groups" and "Modifying Permission Groups" sections later in this chapter for more information.

To assign permissions to a group:

1. Choose Edit > Administer Websites (Contribute > Administer Websites), and then choose the Web site you want to administer from the cascading menu.

   The Administrator Password dialog appears.

2. Type the password and click OK.

   The Administer Website dialog appears (**Figure 10.12**).

3. In the "Permission groups" section of the dialog, select the group for which you want to assign permissions (**Figure 10.13**).

   continues on next page

ASSIGNING PERMISSIONS

4. Click Edit Group.

The Permission Group dialog appears (**Figure 10.14**).

5. Select a category from the list on the left side of the Permission Group dialog.

The right side of the Permission Group dialog changes to reflect your choice.

6. Make changes to the permissions in the category you selected.

For details on each of the permissions within each category, see the discussion of each category below.

7. (Optional) If you wish, select another category, and then make changes to those permissions. Repeat until you're finished.

8. Click OK to save your changes to the permission group and return to the Administer Website dialog.

9. Click OK to save your permission changes to the server.

Permission categories   Permissions

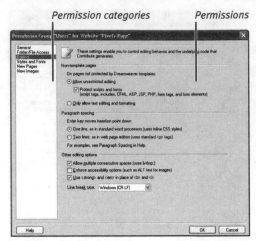

Figure 10.14 The Permission Group dialog has several categories, each with a number of permissions you can set.

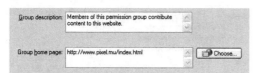

Figure 10.15 The General category contains information for permission-group members and sets the home page for the group.

General permissions

The first item in this category provides information for prospective group members, and the second sets the home page for the group (**Figure 10.15**).

◆ **Group description** is a field where you can clearly describe the responsibilities and permissions available for the group.

◆ **Group home page** allows you to choose a specific page within the Web site to be the initial page for the group, and that page can be different from the site's main home page. For example, if the home page of your site is `http://www.backupbrain.com/index.html`, and you want the sales team to default to the sales portion of the site, you enter the URL `http:// www.backupbrain.com/sales/index.html` in the "Group home page" field. You can also use the Browse button next to the "Group home page" field to find the home page you want.

Folder/File Access permissions

These settings allow you to specify the folders to which users have access, as well as assign ability to delete files on the site.

◆ **Folder access** settings let you give users permission to edit files in any folder on the Web site, or restrict them to editing only in specified folders (**Figure 10.16**). The default is to allow users to edit files in any folder. If you want to restrict folder access, select "Only allow editing within these folders," and then click Add Folder, which brings up the Choose Folder dialog. Navigate to the folder you want users to be able to edit, and then click the Select button, which returns you to the Permission Group dialog and adds the selected folder to the folder list. Repeat as necessary to add other folders. To change one of the folders in the list, select it, and then click Edit or Remove.

◆ **File deletion** settings control whether users can delete files they can edit (**Figure 10.17**). The default is to prevent users from deleting files and allow only members of the Administrator group to delete files. To enable file deletion for users, select "Allow users to delete files they have permission to edit" This also enables the "Remove rollback versions on delete" option. You must select this option if you want your users to have the ability to delete files.

✔ Tip

■ Remember that Contribute permissions are in *addition* to the server permission settings. If you do not have server permissions to delete a file, Contribute will not allow the file to be deleted, no matter what the user group setting is.

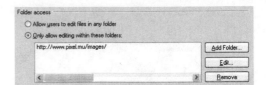

Figure 10.16 The "Folder access" section of the Folder/File Access permissions category lets you specify which folders users can access to edit files.

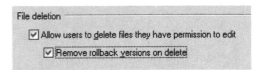

Figure 10.17 You can control whether users can delete files from the site.

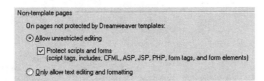

Figure 10.18 The "Non-template pages" section of the Editing permissions category controls what users can accomplish on non-Dreamweaver pages.

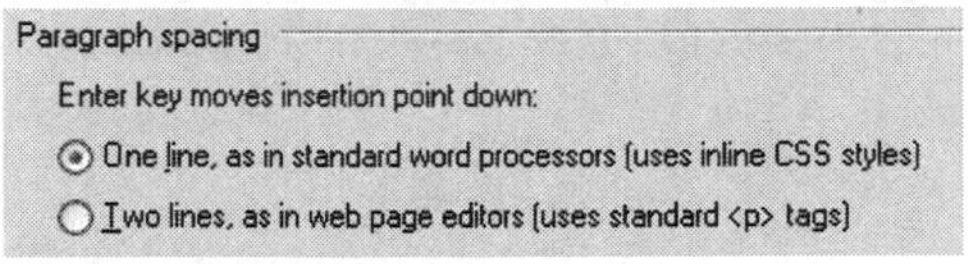

Figure 10.19 You can control paragraph spacing using either CSS styles (the preferred method) or HTML tags.

Editing permissions

Editing permissions control the actions users can take on nontemplate pages, how Contribute creates paragraph breaks, and other miscellaneous editing options.

◆ **Non-template pages** settings control options for pages that aren't created from Dreamweaver templates (**Figure 10.18**). By default, Contribute is set to "Allow unrestricted editing" and "Protect scripts and forms." The first option lets users insert and modify anything on a Contribute page, including text, images, tables, Flash movies, and more. The exception is controlled by the second option, which prevents users from deleting script tags, code tags (such as instructions for Macromedia ColdFusion or ASP tags), and form elements. If you deselect this option, users can modify code embedded in your Web pages. Most Contribute users will not have the knowledge or experience to change code safely, and the tools for code modification are far superior in Dreamweaver. In general, it's best to leave the Web programming to Dreamweaver users.

◆ The "**Only allow text editing and formatting**" option restricts users to editing text, modifying styles, and creating bulleted or numbered lists. Users cannot add images, links, Flash movies, or tables.

◆ **Paragraph spacing** settings control the Contribute behavior when the user presses Enter (Return) (**Figure 10.19**). The default uses CSS styles and moves the insertion point down one line when the user presses Enter (Return). The other option moves the insertion point down two lines and uses HTML <p> tags. For a detailed explanation of the effects of these controls, see the "That's the Breaks" sidebar in Chapter 4.

◆ **Other editing options** include four miscellaneous options (**Figure 10.20**). **Allow multiple consecutive spaces** uses the HTML   character (a nonbreaking space) to allow the user to insert multiple consecutive spaces between words. Contribute enables this option by default. When you disable it, browsers collapse multiple spaces into only one space.

◆ The **Enforce accessibility options** choice is turned off by default, but I suggest you turn it on. When it is on, Contribute always prompts users for information that will make it easier for people with disabilities to access your Web site. For example, when the user inserts an image, Contribute prompts the user to provide a text description for the image (also known as ALT text), which can be read by screen readers used by site visitors with visual disabilities (**Figure 10.21**). This option does not require users to specify header elements for tables (although to learn how to employ proper accessibility, see Chapter 7, "Creating Tables," for more information about table header elements).

◆ The **Use <strong> and <em> in place of <b> and <i>** option tells Contribute to use more up-to-date HTML when users format text as bold or italic. This option is turned on by default.

◆ The **Line break type** pop-up menu allows you to specify the invisible Windows, Macintosh, or Unix line-break characters. Contribute defaults to Windows line breaks, but the line breaks used should be compatible with the type of line breaks your Web server understands. Check with your site administrator if you have questions.

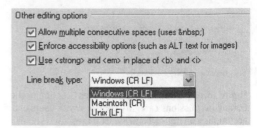

Figure 10.20 The miscellaneous editing options include the important ability to enforce accessibility requirements for site visitors with visual disabilities.

Figure 10.21 If you have enabled accessibility enforcement, Contribute presents this dialog whenever you add an image to your Web site.

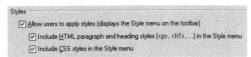

Figure 10.22 The Styles section of the Styles and Fonts permissions category controls whether or not the user can apply text styles.

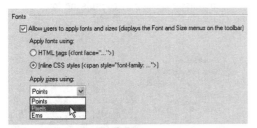

Figure 10.23 The Fonts section of the Styles and Fonts permissions category controls the user's ability to apply fonts and font sizes.

Styles and Fonts permissions

Styles and Fonts permissions control users' ability to apply text styles and define the kinds of text styles they can use. You can also allow or disallow users to specify fonts and font sizes.

◆ **Styles** has the "Allow users to apply styles" option turned on by default (**Figure 10.22**). Contribute also enables the two subsidiary options by default and allows HTML paragraph and heading styles and CSS styles to appear in the Style menu.

◆ **Fonts** lets you enable or disable the Font and Font Size menus on the Editing toolbar. Contribute enables this option by default. If you allow users to apply fonts and sizes, you have the further option of specifying whether fonts should be applied using HTML tags or CSS styles (**Figure 10.23**). If you choose CSS styles, you have the additional option of using points, pixels, or ems as the measurement unit.

✔ Tips

■ You can prevent a CSS custom class from being available to Contribute users by naming the style with the prefix mmhide. The style will not appear in the Style menu. For example, if you use a style named Slugline in your page, but you don't want Contribute users to be able to use that style, rename it mmhideSlugline.

■ You have the most control over the contributor's use of text on the site if you deselect "Allow users to apply fonts and sizes" and specify CSS styles within the editable regions on the template. On the other hand, this option is so restrictive that your users may revolt.

ASSIGNING PERMISSIONS

205

New Pages permissions

The New Pages settings control the kind of Web pages users can create from the New Page dialog.

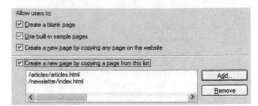

Figure 10.24 The "Allow users to" section of the New Pages permissions category controls the source of new pages in the New Page dialog.

- ◆ **Allow users to** has three self-explanatory options that are enabled by default (**Figure 10.24**). They are "Create a blank page," "Use built-in sample pages," and "Create a new page by copying any page on the website." When you select the "Create a new page by copying a page from this list" option, you can add or subtract pages from your Web site that can be used like Sample Pages, although they will appear in the Templates category of the New Page dialog. Use the Add button to add pages from your Web site to the list. You can use pages only from the current Web site; you can't select pages from any of your other Web sites for this list.

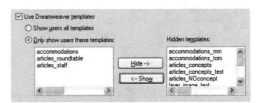

Figure 10.25 You can restrict users to certain Dreamweaver templates.

- ◆ **Use Dreamweaver templates** is enabled by default, as is its subsidiary option "Show users all templates." You also have the option of restricting the templates users can see by clicking the "Only show users these templates" button and moving templates from the "Hidden templates" list, using the Hide and Show buttons (**Figure 10.25**).

✔ Tips

- ■ By restricting the Dreamweaver templates that members of a group can see, you can prevent members of one department from accidentally using templates meant for another department. For example, by restricting templates for the public relations group to the templates designed for press releases, you can make sure the PR group doesn't accidentally use progress reports templates meant for the engineering group.

- ■ If you don't like the Sample Pages that Macromedia provides with Contribute, you can prevent your users from accessing them by deselecting the "Use built-in sample pages" option.

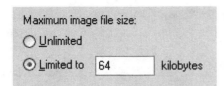

Figure 10.26 Limit the maximum size of images that users can add to your site in the New Images category of the Permission Group dialog.

New Images permissions

The New Images category lets you restrict the maximum file size of images that users can add to the site's pages.

- ◆ **Maximum image file size** can be set to Unlimited, or you can type a number, in kilobytes, in the "Limited to" field (**Figure 10.26**).

✔ Tips

- ■ When you set the maximum image file size permission to 0, users can't insert images. This setting is useful when you want users to be able to change text but not add graphics to the Web site.

- ■ Using a relatively low number for the maximum image file size prevents users from adding individual images to your site that are too big for site visitors using dial-up connections to load in a reasonable amount of time. The setting restricts the size of a single image, not the aggregated size of all the images on the page.

Creating Permission Groups

You're not limited to the two default groups Contribute provides; you can create new groups as you need them. After you, as the site administrator, create permission groups, you'll need to send connection keys to your users. See "Sharing Site Connections" in Chapter 2 for more information.

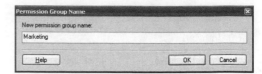

Figure 10.27 Name the new permission group.

To create a new permission group:

1. Choose Edit > Administer Websites (Contribute > Administer Websites), and then choose the Web site you want to administer from the cascading menu.

   The Administrator Password dialog appears.

2. Type the password and click OK.

   The Administer Website dialog appears.

3. Click New.

   The Permission Group Name dialog appears (**Figure 10.27**).

4. Type a name for the new group, and then click OK.

   You return to the Administer Website dialog, and the name of the new group appears in the dialog.

5. Select the new permission group in the list, and then click Edit Group.

6. Edit the group permissions as described in the "To assign permissions to a group" section earlier in this chapter.

✔ Tip

■ Individual permission groups don't have passwords, so a single user cannot be a member of more than one permission group. Users join a permission group by using the connection key sent to them by the site administrator.

Modifying Permission Groups

You can modify the editing privileges for groups, delete groups, or duplicate groups to use as the basis for new groups.

Because Contribute stores the permission-group settings in the *shared settings file* on the server, and each copy of Contribute reads that file when it starts up, you can change the permissions for any group at any time without having to send new connection keys to all the group members. You will, however, need to send users a new connection key if you move them into a different group.

✔ Tip

■ Contribute stores the shared settings file in a folder called _mm that resides at the root of the Web site. You can't see this folder from within Contribute.

To edit a permission group:

1. Choose Edit > Administer Websites (Contribute > Administer Websites), and then choose the Web site you want to administer from the cascading menu.
   The Administrator Password dialog appears.

2. Type the password and click OK.
   The Administer Website dialog appears.

3. Select a permission group in the list, and then click Edit Group.

4. Edit the group permissions as described in the "To assign permissions to a group" section earlier in this chapter.

To duplicate a permission group:

1. Choose Edit > Administer Websites (Contribute > Administer Websites), and then choose the Web site you want to administer from the cascading menu.

   The Administrator Password dialog appears.

2. Type the password and click OK.

   The Administer Website dialog appears.

3. Select a permission group in the list, and then click Duplicate.

   The Permission Group Name dialog appears.

4. Type a name for the new group, and then click OK.

   You return to the Administer Website dialog.

5. To edit the new group permissions, click Edit Group, and then edit the permissions as described earlier in this chapter.

✔ Tip

- Duplicating a group is useful if you have groups with similar but not identical permissions. For example, you might have two groups that need the same editing access but use a different template. You can create and tweak the permissions for the first group, then duplicate that group and only change the template sets for the second group. It's a big time-saver.

To delete a permission group:

1. Choose Edit > Administer Websites (Contribute > Administer Websites), and then choose the Web site you want to administer from the cascading menu.

   The Administrator Password dialog appears.

2. Type the password and click OK.

   The Administer Website dialog appears.

3. Select a permission group in the list, and then click Delete.

   Contribute asks you to confirm the deletion (**Figure 10.28**).

4. Click Yes.

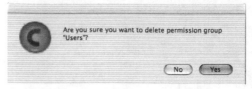

Figure 10.28 Before you delete a permission group, Contribute asks if that's what you want to do.

✔ Tips

- Be careful when you delete a permission group—you can't undo the delete action.

- Contribute doesn't offer a way to remove a single user from a permission group. A workaround is to duplicate the group with a new name, send new connection keys to the users you want to include in the new group, and then delete the old group.

MANAGING SITES WITH DREAMWEAVER

Macromedia designed Contribute around the principle that one or more site administrators will organize and maintain a Web site. Often these administrators used a production tool such as Macromedia Dreamweaver MX to create and prepare the Web site so that content creators could then use Contribute in their work on the site.

Beginning with Dreamweaver MX 6.1, Macromedia built the tools to administer Contribute sites into Dreamweaver, so you can create and administer the site entirely within Dreamweaver. For the most part, these tools replicate the site-administration abilities built into Contribute, which are detailed in Chapter 10, "Site Administration." In this chapter, you learn how to update Dreamweaver MX to administer Contribute; how to create a Contribute-friendly site structure in Dreamweaver; how to become the administrator of a Contribute site with Dreamweaver; and how to use Contribute-style rollbacks from Dreamweaver to revert to previous versions of pages on your site.

Updating Dreamweaver for Contribute

You must be running Dreamweaver MX version 6.1 or later to work with Contribute sites. You can download an updater on the Macromedia Web site (www.macromedia.com/downloads/). Versions of the updater are available for both Windows and Macintosh. Naturally, all new copies of Dreamweaver MX are the updated version.

Figure 11.1 Check your version of Dreamweaver MX to make sure it is compatible with Contribute.

The 6.1 updater adds three Contribute-related features to Dreamweaver:

◆ The capability to administer Contribute sites from within Dreamweaver

◆ The capability to create and send connection keys to Contribute users

◆ The Contribute page-versioning system, which allows you to roll back pages to previous versions, just as you can with Contribute

If you purchased Dreamweaver after December 2002, you should check to see whether you are running a Contribute-compatible version.

To check your version of Dreamweaver MX:

1. Launch Dreamweaver MX.

2. Choose Help > About Dreamweaver (Windows) or Dreamweaver > About Macromedia Dreamweaver MX (Macintosh).
   The Dreamweaver credits screen appears.

3. Click the credits screen once.
   The version screen appears (**Figure 11.1**). If the version shown is 6.0, you need to download and apply the updater in order to work with Contribute from Dreamweaver.

4. Click the version screen once to dismiss it.

To update Dreamweaver MX:

1. Download the appropriate updater for your computer (either Windows or Macintosh) from Macromedia's Web site at www.macromedia.com/downloads/.

2. Double-click the updater program to launch it.

   The updater program searches your hard drive for an older version of Dreamweaver MX, and, after finding the version, prompts you to complete the update.

3. When the update is completed, exit the updater program.

✔ Tips

■ Have a fast Internet connection or a lot of time before you download the Dreamweaver updater program—the Windows updater is almost 15 MB, and the Mac updater weighs in at almost 26 MB.

■ Be sure to disable all extensions in Dreamweaver MX before installing the version 6.1 updater. Use the Extension Manager to do the job by choosing Commands > Manage Extensions from within Dreamweaver. If you install the updater while Dreamweaver MX extensions are enabled, the extensions disappear from the Dreamweaver menus. After you install the updater and start Dreamweaver MX 6.1 for the first time, use the Extension Manager to reenable your extensions.

■ The version 6.1 updater also fixes a long list of bugs (some minor, some not so) that Macromedia discovered in Dreamweaver 6.0, so it's a good thing to install even if you don't plan to administer Contribute sites from Dreamweaver. For a list of the Dreamweaver bugs fixed by the updater, check the Release Notes section of the Macromedia Dreamweaver Support Center on the Macromedia Web site.

UPDATING DREAMWEAVER FOR CONTRIBUTE

Building Sites for Contribute

Many Contribute site administrators are also the designers or developers. If you are the administrator, you can do a variety of things to make using your sites easier for content creators.

Preparing a Contribute-friendly site structure

It's a good idea to review your site structure and make any changes necessary to facilitate the creation of permission groups before you deploy Contribute to your content creators. For example, you might have a Web site with many contributors whose content doesn't affect the content of other users, such as a faculty Web site in which each faculty member can update information about his or her class schedule, office hours, and so on. For such a site, creating and designating a separate folder for each faculty member might be appropriate. When you create the permissions for the site, you have a few options. You could create a single permission group in Contribute for all faculty members and use the server file system to limit their server access so that each faulty member could read and write to files only in his or her own folder. This approach works well if you have many contributors; the Contribute built-in permissions management doesn't scale well when you have dozens or hundreds of contributors. If you want to handle access entirely within Contribute, you could create a separate Contribute permission group for each faculty member, specifying the folder he or she has access to in the Folder Access setting in the File/Folder Access category of the Permission Group dialog. Either way, such a site would have a single administrator, single shared-settings file, and a shared set of Dreamweaver templates (if the site uses Dreamweaver templates).

Contribute could also be deployed in sites with multiple administrators, one for each section of the site. Each administrator would set up his or her section for his or her Contribute users. For example, a company could have a different section (and a different administrator) for the sales department, the human resources department, the manufacturing group, and customer service. Each department would have its own folder, and each department could have its own set of Dreamweaver templates in the Templates folder within its section folder. The benefit of this approach would be that all the users in all the departments could browse the full site, but they would be restricted to editing only pages within their folders.

Building standards compliance into the site

Contribute shares the excellent Dreamweaver MX HTML-creation engine, a hidden bonus. You can create Web sites that are completely compliant with Web standards, as long as the designer has taken care to create compliant templates. Web standards help ensure that everyone has access to the information on your Web sites, make the browsing experience faster and more enjoyable, and also make life easier for Web designers and developers.

Standards compliance facilitates the use of the Web by people with special needs; the degree to which people with disabilities can fully use a site is referred to as its *accessibility*. On a standards-compliant Web site, blind people can have a computer read the Web pages. People with poor eyesight can have pages magnified for easier reading. The nondisabled also derive benefits—compliant sites enable people using handheld devices, such as PDAs or cell phones, to browse the Web as easily as users sitting at a desktop computer. And compliant sites are easier for search engines to access, evaluate, and index, making for better search results for your site.

continues on next page

BUILDING SITES FOR CONTRIBUTE

Besides these practical reasons, there's another reason you might want to build standards-compliant Web sites. With the adoption of government-backed accessibility standards in the United States, the European Union, Canada, Australia, and Japan, accessibility might not just be a good idea—it could be the law.

Contribute offers several settings that allow designers and Contribute site administrators to establish and maintain accessibility. Once administrators have activated these settings, content creators must provide text descriptions for images (also known as ALT text). Contribute users can also easily identify the headings in tables used for tabular data. The administrator can also specify the use of CSS for text formatting. For more information about these accessibility settings, refer to "Other editing options" in the "Editing permissions" section and the "Styles and Fonts permissions" section in Chapter 10.

Dreamweaver MX has a wide variety of tools to help the page designer create standards-compliant, accessible templates that can then be used in Contribute:

◆ You'll find more than two dozen accessible templates built into Dreamweaver in the Page Designs (Accessible) category of the New Document dialog (**Figure 11.2**).

◆ Dreamweaver also has accessibility preferences; refer to the Dreamweaver documentation for more information.

◆ The Macromedia Accessibility page, at www.macromedia.com/macromedia/accessibility/, has a great deal of information on accessibility and Web standards, and many megabytes of additional accessible templates, free for the downloading.

◆ Dreamweaver offers several extensions that can help you evaluate Web pages and modify them to be more usable and accessible. You can find links to these extensions on the Macromedia Accessibility page.

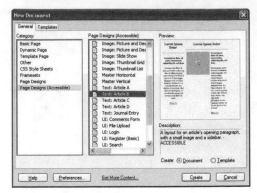

Figure 11.2 Dreamweaver comes with many accessible page designs.

✔ Tip

■ The Sample Pages you find in the Contribute New Page dialog are all accessible, but they are not all standards-compliant (meaning that they do not necessarily pass as valid HTML when using the W3C HTML validator).

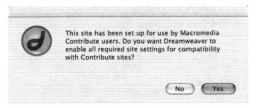

Figure 11.3 When you're working in Dreamweaver and you access for the first time a site that Contribute users have worked on, Dreamweaver asks if you want to enable Contribute compatibility. (In this case, I accessed and administered the Contribute site using Dreamweaver MX in Mac OS X.)

Figure 11.4 You need to identify yourself as a Contribute user by entering your Check Out Name and email address.

Enabling Dreamweaver Settings for Contribute

If Contribute has previously used your remote site, Dreamweaver MX automatically detects that fact when it first connects to the site and asks if you want to enable Contribute compatibility (**Figure 11.3**). If you do, Dreamweaver changes a number of settings in the program and on the site. The program also shows the Contribute Site Settings dialog, which asks for your name and email address as a Contribute user (**Figure 11.4**).

When you fill out this dialog, be sure to choose a different check-in/check-out name for Dreamweaver than the one you use in Contribute so that both Contribute and Dreamweaver can keep correct track of who is editing a page. If you're not familiar with the Dreamweaver terminology, the check-in/check-out name is the name that Dreamweaver (and now, Contribute) uses to identify the people who work on pages in a site. Because both Dreamweaver and Contribute check pages out of a site while they are being edited, you want to be able to keep track of which application has a page checked out.

Both the user name and email address are significant, because they are used together to create a unique user identity. If you prefer, you can use a different user name but the same email address in both applications. By utilizing different user names and having them be descriptive, you can immediately tell which application you used to check out the page. For example, I could set up my sites using "tom-dw" (for Dreamweaver) and "tom-con" (for Contribute), but the same email address (webteam@negrino.com).

continues on next page

Then, if I have a page checked out in Dreamweaver and browse to that page in Contribute, Contribute notifies me in its info bar that the page cannot be edited because it is checked out by "tom-dw <webteam@negrino.com >". I can use a single email address and still immediately know which program has the file in use.

You can see the settings Dreamweaver changes in the Contribute category of the Site Definition dialog (**Figure 11.5**). Here, Dreamweaver has enabled Contribute compatibility and automatically entered the URL of the site root. Dreamweaver also has a button to open the Site Administration dialog, which is identical to the dialog of the same name in Contribute.

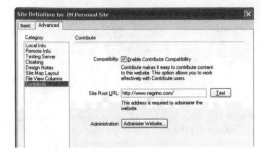

Figure 11.5 After you enable Contribute compatibility, Dreamweaver makes changes in the Contribute category of the Site Definition dialog.

✔ Tips

- You can extend the user names you use in Contribute and Dreamweaver to identify the different machines you use, as well as the different applications. For example, if you use Contribute on both your laptop and your desktop machine, you could have the user names "tom-con-laptop" and "tom-con-desktop."

- You can use the Test button in the Contribute category of the Site Definition dialog to verify that the URL is correct, whether you've entered it manually or Dreamweaver entered it automatically. Dreamweaver connects to the Web site and verifies that it has the correct URL to administer the site.

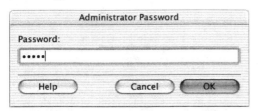

Figure 11.6 Enter the site administrator password to begin creating a connection key.

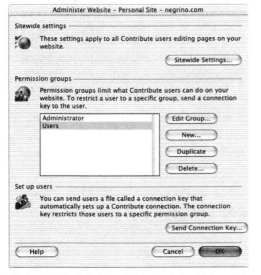

Figure 11.7 The Administer Website dialog looks much the same either in Windows or on the Macintosh (shown here).

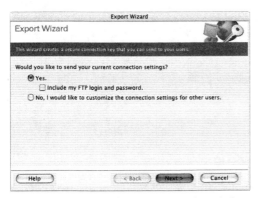

Figure 11.8 The Export Wizard steps you through the process for creating and sending connection keys.

Sharing Connection Keys

As a Dreamweaver user, you're quite likely to be the Contribute site administrator, so you need to know how to send connection keys to Contribute users. The process of sending connection keys is almost the same as it is in Contribute, with minor differences, depending on whether you're using the Windows or the Macintosh version of Dreamweaver MX.

Unfortunately, Dreamweaver MX does not import Contribute connection keys, so you can't use Contribute connection information to add Dreamweaver users to your Web site. Also, Dreamweaver users cannot be assigned to a group and doesn't offer a way to restrict editing access, template access, or Web-site folder access for a Dreamweaver user.

To send connection keys from Dreamweaver:

1. From the menu bar in the Site window, choose Site > Administer Contribute Site (Windows) or Site > Administer Contribute Site (Mac).

   The Administrator Password dialog opens (**Figure 11.6**).

2. Enter the password, and click OK.

   The Administer Website dialog opens (**Figure 11.7**)

3. Click the Send Connection Key button.

   The first screen of the Export Wizard appears (**Figure 11.8**).

4. Make sure that Yes is selected, and then click Next.

   (Optional) Select the "Include my FTP login and password" check box. If you want to include your log-in information in the key, select this box; if the person to whom you're sending the key has his or her own FTP log-in, leave this option deselected.

continues on next page

If you choose No, Contribute allows you to customize the connection settings before you create the export file. See Chapter 10, "Site Administration," for more information about customizing connection settings.

The Group Information screen appears.

5. Select the permission group you want for the connection file you're creating, and then click Next.

The Connection Key Information screen opens.

6. Choose whether to send the connection file in an email or save it to disk (Mac users can't send the file in an email from within Dreamweaver; they can only save connection keys to disk, from which they can be manually attached to an outgoing email). Then enter the password or pass phrase for the connection file, repeat it for verification, and click Next.

Contribute encrypts the connection file with the password or pass phrase so that no one can open it except the intended recipient. The Summary screen of the Export Wizard appears, allowing you to review the information.

7. If you need to make changes, click Back. Otherwise, click Done.

8. If you chose to send the connection key by email (only in Windows), Contribute launches your email program and creates a new message with the connection key as an attachment, the subject already filled in, and the instructions in the body of the message. Address the message, make any other changes you want, and send the mail on its way.

or

If you chose to save the connection key to disk, the Export Connection Key dialog appears (**Figure 11.9**). Choose the location on your hard drive or local network for the connection key, and click Save.

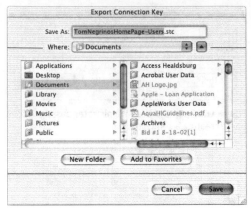

Figure 11.9 Macintosh users have only the option to save connection keys to disk; they can't send them via email.

✔ **Tip**

■ Make sure that you also send the connection key password to the recipient. It's a good idea to send the password in a separate email.

SHARING CONNECTION KEYS

Figure 11.10 On Dreamweaver MX for Windows, you find the Site window in the Files panel group.

Figure 11.11 Dreamweaver MX for Macintosh has a stand-alone Site window.

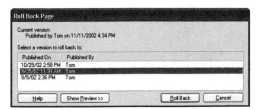

Figure 11.12 The Roll Back Page dialog lets you choose previous versions of your Web pages, which you can then republish to your Web site.

Using Contribute Rollback in Dreamweaver

As detailed in Chapter 3, "Building Web Pages," and Chapter 10, "Site Administration," Contribute has the ability to roll back pages on your Web sites to previously published versions. Site administrators can enable or disable rollback for permission groups of users. Dreamweaver MX can also roll back pages from Contribute users or other Dreamweaver MX users.

You use the Dreamweaver Site window to manage files and folders on your site. Dreamweaver can show the local copy of the site on your machine, as well as the remote copy on the Web server. In this respect, it works differently from Contribute, which always browses and accesses files on the server, and makes local copies of pages only when you are working on draft pages.

In the Windows version of Dreamweaver MX, the Site window is part of the Files panel group (**Figure 11.10**). On the Macintosh, the Site window is a stand-alone window but works almost exactly the same way (**Figure 11.11**).

To roll back to a previous page version:

1. In the Site window, on either the local site or the remote site, select the page you want to roll back.

2. From the menu bar at the top of the Site window, choose File > Roll Back Page (Windows), or choose Roll Back Page from the Site pop-up menu (Macintosh).

   Dreamweaver gets the version information for the page from the server and displays the Roll Back Page dialog (**Figure 11.12**). If the page has no previous versions or the previously published version was created outside of Contribute or Dreamweaver, the Roll Back Page dialog tells you.

continues on next page

3. From the list of versions, choose a previous version.

4. (Optional) If you want to confirm that the version you selected is the one you want, click Show Preview.

The Roll Back Page dialog expands to show you the preview (Windows), or the page opens in your system's default browser (Macintosh). If it's not the version you want, select another in the Roll Back Page dialog.

5. Click Roll Back.

Dreamweaver replaces the currently published version of the page with the previously published version.

✔ Tips

■ When you roll back to a previously published version of a page, Dreamweaver saves the current version on the server as a rollback version, and you can revert to it if you wish.

■ Like Contribute, Dreamweaver can roll back "only" 99 versions of a given page, though the prudent site administrator will probably set far fewer rollback versions to be saved on the Web server.

■ Dreamweaver users can roll back pages changed by Contribute users or Dreamweaver users, and either Dreamweaver or Contribute can roll back pages modified in Dreamweaver .

■ If you have a file checked out (using the Dreamweaver check-in/check-out feature), you must check the file in before you can roll it back to a previous version.

■ If someone else has checked the file out (or is editing it with Contribute), you cannot edit it or roll it back until he or she is done and has released the file.

■ The Dreamweaver Roll Back Page dialog is resizable in Windows but not on the Macintosh. On both platforms, however, you can drag the border between the columns to the right or left to make more room for the information in the columns.

CUSTOMIZING CONTRIBUTE

Macromedia Contribute does a fine job straight out of the box, but like many of the Macromedia programs, it can be customized and extended. For example, you can add your own Sample Pages, which contributors can use from the New Page dialog. You can customize the Contribute Welcome screen with your organization's logo. You can modify and rearrange the Contribute menus so that they are more to your liking, and you can add or change the commands on the menus. Similarly, you can customize the Contribute toolbars. And if you have special instructions or tutorials for your users, you can add topics to the Contribute How Do I panel.

Fair warning—geeky stuff ahead: Unlike the operations covered in the rest of this book, customizing Contribute often means working with a text editor; and for most tasks, you need some knowledge of HTML, JavaScript, and XML, and that means getting your hands dirty with some code. On the other hand, some quite useful ways of customizing Contribute require little or no coding, and I'll show you those, too.

A complete discussion of customizing and extending Contribute is beyond the scope of this book, but in this chapter I'll point you toward some resources that help you learn more.

Understanding Contribute Extensibility

Like the Dreamweaver MX interface, the Contribute user interface is written in a combination of HTML, JavaScript, and XML. In fact, virtually everything you see and work with in Contribute is an *extension* written in one of these languages and stored in the Contribute Configuration folder (more about that folder later). Advanced Contribute users and site administrators can customize Contribute using Dreamweaver MX or a simple text editor, such as Notepad (though you'll probably want a more robust tool). If you're familiar with the extensibility of other Macromedia products, such as Flash MX, Fireworks MX, or especially Dreamweaver MX, you'll find Contribute's extensibility to be familiar but maybe also a bit frustrating. That's because Contribute uses conventions and procedures for extensibility similar to those in Dreamweaver, but Contribute is somewhat more limited in scope and, for the end user, is not as convenient as Dreamweaver in this regard.

The standard mechanism for extending other programs in the MX product line is to use the Macromedia Extension Manager, a program that installs prepackaged extensions you download from the Macromedia Exchange site, an online clearinghouse for extensions, or other Web sites. (You can reach the Macromedia Exchange site by choosing Help > Dreamweaver Exchange while in Dreamweaver.) The Extension Manager is necessary because installing the different parts of an extension in the correct places to work with the Macromedia programs can be tricky.

With the introduction of Contribute 2.0, Macromedia has shared the necessary information with developers to allow them to extend Contribute. In fact, the PayPal ecommerce features discussed in Chapter 4 is actually an extension written by a company named WebAssist (http://www.webassist.com). Unfortunately, Contribute 2.0 and older still do not support the Extension Manager, although future versions of Contribute probably will. As a result, if you want to customize and extend Contribute, you have to do it manually or leave adding extensions to developers.

You can download *Extending Contribute*, a book in Adobe Acrobat form, from the Contribute Designer and Developer Center, at http://www.macromedia.com/devnet/contribute/. This book details the similarities and differences between extending Contribute and extending Dreamweaver.

You also can create your own extensions, such as dialogs, menu commands, and so on, using a combination of HTML, JavaScript, and XML. You need a considerable amount of experience with these languages, as well as a good understanding of how to make Dreamweaver extensions. For more information on that lengthy subject, see the online book *Extending Dreamweaver*, which you can access by choosing Help > Extending Dreamweaver from within Dreamweaver MX. You might also find it useful to download *Customizing Macromedia Dreamweaver MX* from the Macromedia Dreamweaver Support Center, at http://www.macromedia.com/support/dreamweaver/.

✔ Tips

- If you need a friendly introduction to JavaScript, I suggest *JavaScript for the World Wide Web: Visual QuickStart Guide, Fifth Edition*, from Peachpit Press, and written by Dori Smith and … uh … me.

- You can find more information on HTML in the excellent *HTML for the World Wide Web, Visual QuickStart Guide, Fifth Edition*, written by Elizabeth Castro and also from Peachpit Press. The same author has also written *XML for the World Wide Web, Visual QuickStart Guide* for Peachpit Press.

- If the online resources at the Macromedia Web site aren't available at the specific URLs above, don't panic; companies are forever changing their Web sites, and you might have to search around a bit to find what you want.

Extension folder structure

As mentioned in the preceding section, the Contribute Configuration folder contains the extensions that come with Contribute. In most cases you will modify files in this folder to customize Contribute.

You can find the Contribute Configuration folder at C:\Program Files\Macromedia\Contribute\ Configuration\ (**Figure 12.1**) on Windows, or at harddrive/Applications/Macromedia Contribute 2/Configuration/ on Macintosh.

Inside the Configuration folder, you'll find many other folders, which contain the files that actually make up the extensions. These folders, such as Commands, Menus, Objects, and Toolbars, make it easy to find the particular files you need to modify in order to customize Contribute. For example, to change the names of menus or the shortcut keys associated with menus, you must edit the file ccmenus.xml inside the Menus folder.

Figure 12.1 The Contribute Configuration folder contains all the extensions that make up the program.

What's Extensible?

Contribute allows you (if you know how) to extend the following features in the same way you extend them in Dreamweaver MX:

◆ Menus, including the ones on the menu bar and the shortcut menus. You need to add new menu items to trigger extensions such as objects or commands.

◆ Toolbars, which can be modified by adding or deleting buttons and other controls; you can also define new toolbars.

◆ Commands, which perform specific tasks. For example, any task invoked from a menu or toolbar is a command. By default, new objects appear at the bottom of the Contribute Format menu.

◆ Objects, which can insert blocks of HTML code or text into the current document. For example, you can define an object that inserts boilerplate text into a page. By default, new objects appear at the bottom of the Contribute Insert menu.

◆ Floating Panels, which are similar to commands but can work interactively while the user edits a page. For example, you can create a floating panel that warns the user when he or she inserts images that are too large.

◆ Translators.

◆ Third Party Tags.

◆ JavaScript Extensions.

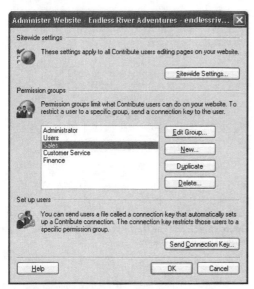

Figure 12.2 Begin the process of saving a page as a Sample Page in the Administer Website dialog.

Creating Sample Pages Templates

One of the most useful customizations you can make to Contribute—adding to the set of Sample Pages that come with Contribute—requires no code modifications. All you need is to be the Contribute site administrator.

Sample Pages are pages on the site that serve as models for new pages but don't have locked and editable regions. Instead, the entire page is editable. Basically, a Sample Page is a regular HTML file that Contribute uses as a starting point for a new page.

You should be aware that after you add a new Sample Page, it appears in the Templates folder of the New Page dialog, not in the Sample Web Pages folder, which is apparently reserved for Macromedia's use. Your content contributors will be able to choose the new Sample Page you added just as they would choose any other template for your site.

Before you begin the following task, you should have already created the page you want to become the Sample Page in Dreamweaver or Contribute.

To add a custom Sample Page:

1. Choose Edit > Administer Websites (Contribute > Administer Websites), and then choose the Web site to which you want to add the sample page from the cascading menu.

   The Administrator Password dialog appears.

2. Enter the administrator password, and click OK.

   The Administer Website dialog appears (**Figure 12.2**).

continues on next page

CREATING SAMPLE PAGES TEMPLATES

3. In the "Permission groups" section of the dialog, select the group that will use the new Sample Page, and then click Edit Group.

 The Permission Group dialog for the selected group appears (**Figure 12.3**).

4. In the category list on the left side of the dialog, click New Pages.

5. In the "Allow users to" section of the dialog, select "Create a new page by copying a page from this list" (**Figure 12.4**).

6. Click Add.

 The Choose File on Website dialog appears (**Figure 12.5**).

7. Navigate to and select the page you want to become the Sample Page.

 A preview of the page appears in the Preview section of the dialog.

8. Click OK.

 You return to the Permission Group dialog, and Contribute adds the page you selected to the list box.

9. Click OK to return to the Administer Website dialog.

10. Click OK to save your administrative changes.

To use your new Sample Page, browse to the site where you want to create the new page, choose File > New Page, or click New Page on the toolbar. Your new Sample Page appears in the Templates folder of the New Page dialog.

✔ Tips

■ When you select pages to become Sample Pages, Contribute restricts you to the Web site associated with the permission group you're modifying; you can't choose from pages on other sites for which you have connections. This is different from some other operations in Contribute where you use the Choose File on Website dialog.

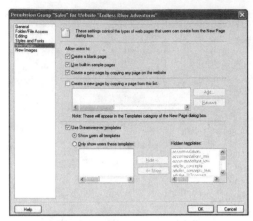

Figure 12.3 Select the New Pages category of the Permission Group dialog.

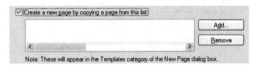

Figure 12.4 After you select "Create a new page by copying a page from this list," the Add and Remove buttons become active.

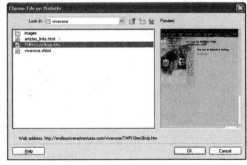

Figure 12.5 Choose the file you want to make into a Sample Page.

■ There's no reason why you can't create Sample Pages in Dreamweaver. However, saving a Sample Page as a Dreamweaver template gives the file a different extension (.dwt). Instead, save Sample Pages in Dreamweaver as regular HTML files.

Figure 12.6 This Mac screen shows the Contribute Welcome screen before any connections have been added. The Windows screen is similar.

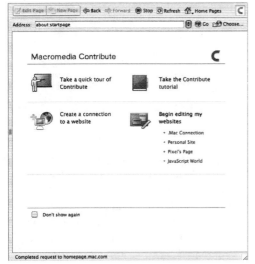

Figure 12.7 After you have made site connections, your Web sites become available on the Welcome screen.

Customizing the Welcome Screen

You can customize the Welcome screen, the screen that users see when they first launch Contribute. You might want to customize it to reflect the logo of your organization. If you're a designer, you can customize the Welcome screen for your clients.

The Welcome screen looks simple (**Figure 12.6**), but it is actually an automatically generated HTML file (`welcome.htm`) based on a Dreamweaver template (`welcome.dwt`). Rather than having the Welcome page be a static HTML page, you can add Contribute connections, and the Welcome page changes to list all your connections (**Figure 12.7**).

To change the Welcome page, you use Dreamweaver to edit the `welcome.dwt` template, located in the `Contribute\Configuration\Content\Welcome\` folder (Windows), or the `Applications/Macromedia Contribute 2/Configuration/Content/Welcome/` folder (Mac). After you edit the template and save your changes, the next time you launch Contribute, it generates a new `welcome.htm` file based on the new template.

To customize the Welcome screen:

1. Quit Contribute.

2. On the Windows desktop, open the `Contribute\Configuration\Content\Welcome\` folder, and make a duplicate of the `welcome.dwt` file so that you have a backup in case anything goes awry.

   or

   On the Mac desktop, open the `Macromedia Contribute 2/Configuration/Content/Welcome/` folder, and make a backup of the `welcome.dwt` file.

continues on next page

3. Launch Dreamweaver.

4. (Windows) Choose File > Open, and then open the file `C:\Program Files\Macromedia Contribute\Configuration\Content\Welcome\welcome.dwt`.

   or

   (Mac) Choose File > Open, and then open the file `Applications/Macromedia Contribute 2/Configuration/Content/Welcome/welcome.dwt`.

   The file opens in Dreamweaver.

5. Make your changes to the template file, and then save and close the template.

   Because the Welcome template is a special template, it doesn't work the way other templates work in Contribute. You should not save it in the Templates folder; instead, save it in the Welcome folder. You also should store any assets for this page, such as CSS files or images, in the Welcome folder.

6. Quit Dreamweaver.

7. Launch Contribute.

   The new Welcome screen appears (**Figure 12.8**).

Figure 12.8 After you modify the template on which the Welcome screen is based, the Welcome screen gains a whole new look.

✔ Tips

- If you want multiple users to be able to use your new Welcome page, you must copy the edited `welcome.dwt` template file to each user's Configuration folder.

- For a more detailed and technical discussion of customizing the Welcome screen, look for the article "Co-Branding Contribute" on the Macromedia Contribute Designer and Development Center site.

- The Welcome screen is one of the features Contribute has that Dreamweaver does not. Another such feature is the Contribute How Do I panel. Like the Welcome screen, it can be customized to allow you to provide online help for your site users. Because the procedure for modifying the How Do I panel is beyond the scope of this book, I suggest you obtain *Extending Contribute*, from the Contribute Designer and Developer Center on the Macromedia Web site.

Customizing Menus

You can change the names of any items in any of the Contribute menus and rearrange the order of items in the menus. Contribute defines all its menus, including the ones in the menu bar and its shortcut menus, in an XML file named ccmenus.xml, in the Contribute\Configuration\Menus\ folder (Windows) or the Macromedia Contribute 2/Configuration/Menus/ folder (Mac). To change the menus, you must use Dreamweaver or a text editor to edit the ccmenus.xml file.

Important! Before you change this file, be sure to quit Contribute and duplicate the ccmenus.xml file under another name so that you have a backup in case you make a mistake in your editing.

To change menu items:

1. Quit Contribute.

2. Launch Dreamweaver or whatever text-editing program you use for editing XML files.

continues on next page

3. (Windows) Choose File > Open, and then open the file `C:\Program Files\ Macromedia Contribute\Configuration\ Menus\ccmenus.xml`.

or

(Mac) Choose File > Open, and then open the file `Applications/Macromedia Contribute 2/Configuration/Content/ Menus/ccmenus.dwt`.

The file opens in Dreamweaver or your other editing program (**Figure 12.9**). The main menu bar for Contribute is toward the end of the file; you can recognize it because it begins with

`<menubar name="Main Window"`
`→ id="DWMainWindow">`

(See the gray arrow in Step 3? Because book pages are narrower than computer screens, some of the lines of code in this chapter are too long to fit on the page. When that happens, we've broken the line into segments, inserted the gray arrow to indicate that it's a continued line, and indented the rest of the line. But when you see the line in your text editor, it should be one long line.)

4. To move a menu or menu item, select it from its opening tag (example: `<menu>`) to its closing tag (example: `</menu>`), cut it, place the insertion point where you want to move it, and then paste.

or

To rename a menu or menu item, find it in the code and then change its `name` attribute.

or

To insert a separator in a menu, type `<separator />` between two `menuitem` tags.

5. Save and close `ccmenus.xml`, and then launch Contribute to see your changes.

✔ Tip

■ Do not change the `ID` attribute of any menu item in the `ccmenus.xml` file, or Contribute might not be able to perform the menu command.

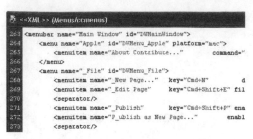

Figure 12.9 This close-up of the ccmenus.xml file shows the beginning of the code for the main menu bar.

Changing Keyboard Shortcuts

You can change keyboard shortcuts for a command if you don't agree with Macromedia's commands.

Important! Before you begin, be sure to quit Contribute and duplicate the `ccmenus.xml` file under another name so that you have a backup in case you make a mistake in your editing.

To change keyboard shortcuts:

1. Quit Contribute.

2. Launch Dreamweaver or whatever text-editing program you use for editing XML files.

3. (Windows) Choose File > Open, and then open the file `C:\Program Files\ Macromedia Contribute\Configuration\ Menus\ccmenus.xml`.

    or

    (Mac) Choose File > Open, and then open the file `Applications/Macromedia Contribute 2/Configuration/Content/ Menus/ccmenus.dwt`.

    The file opens in Dreamweaver or your other editing program. The main menu bar for Contribute is toward the end of the file; you can recognize it because it begins with

    ```
    <menubar name="Main Window"
    → id="DWMainWindow">
    ```

    continues on next page

Syntax of the menus.xml File

The `menus.xml` file is, like all XML files, a highly structured file. It contains a list of menu bars, menus, menu items, keyboard shortcuts, shortcut lists, and separators. The items are described using XML tags. Here's a simplified syntax for the tags that make up the `menus.xml` file:

◆ The `<menubar>` tag provides information about a menu bar in the Contribute menu structure. The tag must contain a `name` and `ID` attribute, and one or more `<menu>` tags.

◆ The `<menu>` tag gives information about a menu or submenu. The `name` attribute is the name of the menu as it will appear in the menu bar. The `<menu>` tag requires an `ID` attribute and can contain one or more `<menuitem>` tags and one or more `<separator>` tags. If the `<menu>` tag contains other `<menu>` tags, those tags become a submenu of the parent `<menu>` tag.

◆ The `<menuitem>` tag defines a menu item. The `<menuitem>` tag must have `name` and `ID` attributes. It can contain the `key` attribute, which defines the keyboard shortcut for the menu item. A `<menuitem>` tag must be contained within a `<menu>` tag.

◆ The `<separator>` tag causes a separator to appear in the menu. The tag has no attributes and must be contained in a `<menu>` tag.

For more details on each of these tags, download *Customizing Macromedia Dreamweaver MX* from the Macromedia Dreamweaver Support Center.

4. If you're reassigning an existing keyboard shortcut (for example, you want to swap the shortcut for Insert Table, which on Windows is is Ctrl-Alt-T, with that of Select Table, which is Ctrl-T), find the menu item to which the shortcut is currently assigned, and change the key attribute.

   For example, you would find the following lines (**Figure 12.10**):

   ```
   <menuitem name="Select Table"
   → key="Cmd+T">
   ```

   and

   ```
   <menu name="Insert"
   → id="DWMenu_Table_Insert">
   <menuitem name="Table"
   → key="Cmd+Opt+T">
   ```

   Then you would swap the code between the quotation marks in the key attributes.

   or

   If you want to add a shortcut key to a menu item that does not currently have one, add key="" anywhere between attributes inside the `<menuitem>` tag. Place the shortcut key between the double quotation marks.

5. Save and close `ccmenus.xml`, and then launch Contribute to see your changes.

✔ Tips

- When changing keyboard commands, make sure you don't accidentally duplicate a keyboard command that is in use elsewhere in the program. If the keyboard shortcut is already being used and you don't remove that use of it, the shortcut will apply only to the first menu item that uses it and will be ignored for the second menu item.

- Underscores in menu or menu-item names indicate the letter in the name to be used for Windows accelerator keys. I've omitted them in the code samples above for clarity.

```
<menu name="T_able" id="DWMenu_Table">
    <menuitem name="_Select Table" key="Cmd+T">
        <menu name="_Insert" id="DWMenu_Table_Insert">
            <menuitem name="_Table"        key="Cmd+Opt+T"
            <separator />
```

Figure 12.10 These lines in the ccmenus.xml file create the Table menu, the Select Table menu item, the Insert menu item, and the Insert > Table submenu item.

Keyboard Command String Equivalents

When assigning keyboard shortcuts, Contribute uses particular strings to denote modifier keys; you use the strings within the key attribute. Because Contribute is derived from Dreamweaver, and Dreamweaver is a cross-platform application, the strings denote different modifier keys on different platforms.

- ◆ Cmd specifies the Control key for Windows or the Command key for Macintosh.

- ◆ Ctrl specifies the Control key for either platform.

- ◆ Shift specifies the Shift key for both platforms.

- ◆ Alt and Opt interchangeably specify the Alt key for Windows or the Option key for Macintosh.

Use the plus sign (+) to separate modifier keys—for example, Cmd+P.

CONTRIBUTE KEYBOARD SHORTCUTS

Macromedia Contribute 2 is easy to use, but you will get your work done even faster if you learn some of the keyboard shortcuts the program uses. If you use Contribute on both Mac and Windows, as I do, you'll be happy to know that most of the shortcut keys are the same between the two versions. Just substitute the Mac's Command (Apple) and Option keys with the Control and Alt keys, respectively, on Windows, and you should have few problems. There are a few features that have Windows shortcut keys with no Mac equivalents, however. Those are listed in the table on the next page.

Table A.1

Contribute Shortcut Keys		
ACTION	MAC SHORTCUT KEY	WINDOWS SHORTCUT KEY
Contribute Menu (Mac only)		
Hide Contribute	Cmd-H	
Hide Others	Cmd-Opt-H	
Quit	Cmd-Q	
File Menu		
Create a new page	Cmd-N	Ctrl-N
Edit page	Cmd-Shift-E	Ctrl-Shift-E
Publish page	Cmd-Shift-P	Ctrl-Shift-P
Save page	Cmd-S	Ctrl-S
Save for later	Cmd-Shift-L	Ctrl-Shift-L
Print	Cmd-P	Ctrl-P
Preview in Browser	N/A	F12
Quit		Ctrl-Q
Edit Menu		
Undo	Cmd-Z	Ctrl-Z
Redo	Cmd-Y	Ctrl-Y
Cut	Cmd-X	Ctrl-X
Copy	Cmd-C	Ctrl-C
Paste	Cmd-V	Ctrl-V
Paste Text Only	Cmd-Shift-V	Ctrl-Shift-V
Select All	Cmd-A	Ctrl-A
Clear	Del	Delete
Find	Cmd-F	Ctrl-F
View Menu		
Open or close Sidebar	N/A	F4
Go to Browser	Cmd-Shift-B	Ctrl-Shift-B
Back in Browser	Opt-Left Arrow	Alt-Left Arrow
Forward in Browser	Opt-Right Arrow	Alt-Right Arrow
Stop loading a page	Esc	Esc
Refresh page	Cmd-R	F5
Go to Web Address	Cmd-O	Ctrl-O
Choose File on Website	Cmd-Shift-O	Ctrl-Shift-O
Insert Menu		
Insert Image From My Computer	Cmd-Opt-I	Ctrl-Alt-I
Insert Table	Cmd-Opt-T	Ctrl-Alt-T
Insert Link from Drafts and Recent Pages	Cmd-Opt-L	Ctrl-Alt-L
Insert Section Anchor	Cmd-Opt-A	Ctrl-Alt-A
Insert Line Break	Shift-Return	Shift-Enter
Insert Non-Breaking Space	Cmd-Shift-Space	Ctrl-Shift-Space

Table A.1

Contribute Shortcut Keys *(continued)*

ACTION	MAC SHORTCUT KEY	WINDOWS SHORTCUT KEY
Format Menu		
Check Spelling	N/A	F7
Bold	Cmd-B	Ctrl-B
Italic	Cmd-I	Ctrl-I
Underline	Cmd-U	Ctrl-U
Align Left	Cmd-Shift-Opt-L	Ctrl-Shift-Alt-L
Align Center	Cmd-Shift-Opt-C	Ctrl-Shift-Alt-C
Align Right	Cmd-Shift-Opt-R	Ctrl-Shift-Alt-R
Justify	Cmd-Shift-Opt-J	Ctrl-Shift-Alt-J
Indent	Cmd-Opt-]	Ctrl-Alt-]
Outdent	Cmd-Opt-[	Ctrl-Alt-[
Set Keywords and Descriptions	Cmd-Opt-K	Ctrl-Alt-K
Set Page Properties	Cmd-J	Ctrl-J
Table Menu		
Select Table	Cmd-T	Ctrl-T
Insert Table	Cmd-Opt-T	Ctrl-Alt-T
Insert Row Above	Cmd-M	Ctrl-M
Insert Column to the Left	Cmd-Shift-A	Ctrl-Shift-A
Merge Cells	Cmd-Opt-M	Ctrl-Alt-M
Split Cell	Cmd-Opt-S	Ctrl-Alt-S
Display Table Properties	Cmd-Shift-T	Ctrl-Shift-T
Help Menu		
Macromedia Contribute Help	Help	F1
Open the Start Page	Opt-Home	Alt-Home
Template Navigation Shortcuts		
Move to the next editable region	Cmd-Opt-E	Ctrl-Alt-E
Move to the previous editable region	Cmd-Shift-Opt-E	Ctrl-Shift-Alt-E

INDEX

R